CW00661390

AIR TRANSPORT AUXILIARY AT WAR

80TH ANNIVERSARY
OF ITS FORMATION

AIR TRANSPORT AUXILIARY AT WAR

80TH ANNIVERSARY OF ITS FORMATION

Stephen Wynn

PEN & SWORD
HISTORY

AN IMPRINT OF PEN & SWORD BOOKS LTD.
YORKSHIRE - PHILADELPHIA

First published in Great Britain in 2021 by
Pen & Sword Military
An imprint of
Pen & Sword Books Limited
Yorkshire - Philadelphia

Copyright © Stephen Wynn, 2021

ISBN 978 1 52672 6 049

The right of Stephen Wynn to be identified as Author of this
work has been asserted by him in accordance
with the Copyright, Designs and Patents Act 1988.

A CIP catalogue record for this book is available from the British Library

All rights reserved. No part of this book may be reproduced or
transmitted in any form or by any means, electronic or mechanical
including photocopying, recording or by any information storage and
retrieval system, without permission from the Publisher in writing.

Typeset in India by IMPEC eSolutions

Printed and bound in the UK
by CPI Group (UK) Ltd, Croydon, CR0 4YY

Pen & Sword Books Limited incorporates the imprints of Atlas,
Archaeology, Aviation, Discovery, Family History, Fiction, History,
Maritime, Military, Military Classics, Politics, Select, Transport,
True Crime, Air World, Frontline Publishing, Leo Cooper,
Remember When, Seaforth Publishing, The Praetorian Press,
Wharncliffe Local History, Wharncliffe Transport,
Wharncliffe True Crime and White Owl.

For a complete list of Pen & Sword titles please contact
PEN & SWORD BOOKS LIMITED
47 Church Street, Barnsley, South Yorkshire S70 2AS, United Kingdom
E-mail: enquiries@pen-and-sword.co.uk
Website: www.pen-and-sword.co.uk
Or
PEN AND SWORD BOOKS
1950 Lawrence Rd, Havertown, PA 19083, USA
E-mail: Uspen-and-sword@casematepublishers.com
Website: www.penandswordbooks.com

About the Author

Stephen is a happily retired police officer having served with Essex Police as a constable for thirty years between 1983 and 2013. He is married to Tanya who is also his best friend.

Both his sons, Luke and Ross, were members of the armed forces, collectively serving five tours in Afghanistan between 2008 and 2013. Both were injured on their first tours. This led to his first book, *Two Sons in a Warzone – Afghanistan: The True Story of a Father's Conflict*, which was published in October 2010.

He also has a teenage daughter, Aimee. Both his grandfathers served in and survived the First World War, one with the Royal Irish Rifles, the other in the Merchant Marine, whilst his father was a member of the Royal Army Ordnance Corps during and after the Second World War.

Stephen collaborated with one of his writing partners, Ken Porter, on a previous book, published in August 2012, *German POW Camp 266 – Langdon Hills*. It spent six weeks as the number one best-selling book in Waterstones, Basildon, between March and April 2013. They have also collaborated on four books in the 'Towns & Cities in the Great War' series by Pen and Sword. Stephen has written other titles for the same series of books and, in February 2017, his book *The Surrender of Singapore – Three Years of Hell 1942-45* was published. This was followed in March 2018 by *Against All Odds: Walter Tull the Black Lieutenant*. October 2018 saw the publication of *Animals in the Great War*; in January 2019 *A History of the Royal Hospital Chelsea – 1682-2017 – The Warriors' Repose* was published. These last two books were written with his wife, Tanya.

Stephen has co-written three crime thrillers which were published between 2010 and 2012 and centre around a fictional detective named Terry Danvers.

When he is not writing, Tanya and he enjoy the simplicity of going out for a coffee and walking their four German Shepherd dogs early each morning when most sensible people are still fast asleep in their beds.

Contents

Jordan Hemmingway, many thanks for leaving your little lights everywhere that you go, they helped me write long into the night. This one's for you.

Introduction

Flying was still in its relative infancy at the outbreak of the Second World War, and it was most certainly only a pastime for the very rich, which made it even more inaccessible for the majority of the public to be able to afford. The man in the street had neither the time nor the money to learn how to fly an aircraft. There would have also been those who would not readily have had the aptitude for it.

The men and women from numerous professions, and from different levels of the middle and upper classes of society, who became members of the Air Transport Auxiliary did so voluntarily. None of them were suitable for service with the Royal Air Force, either because of medical conditions or being simply too old to be considered for wartime military service. Some were thrill-seekers who just had a thing for speed, whether that was racing cars or motorbikes, speedboats in the sea, or private civilian aircraft in the air. The one thing that they all had in common was the desire to do their bit for the country in its hour of need.

It wasn't just British men and women who enlisted. There were men and women from America, Canada, New Zealand, Australia and Poland.

This book looks at the men and women who served in the Air Transport Auxiliary. This includes some of the more well-known individuals as well as some not so well known who served throughout the years of the war. As in all sections of society, groups are made up of numerous individuals who all have a story to tell in one way, shape or form. This includes the guy who had lost one of his arms in a flying accident that was so bad, quite frankly, I find it hard to comprehend how he actually survived the crash, so serious was his list of numerous injuries.

Those who died whilst in the service of the Air Transport Auxiliary are commemorated at a number of different locations around the country, including airfields at Hamble, Ratcliffe, Ringway, Whitchurch and White Waltham. There is also another memorial to them in the crypt area at St Paul's Cathedral in the City of London.

In September 2008, at a ceremony at 10 Downing Street, London, all the surviving veterans of the Air Transport Auxiliary were awarded a special Veteran's Badge by the then Prime Minister, Gordon Brown.

The men and women of the Air Transport Auxiliary did an outstanding job – even more so those who were not British but who still wanted to do their bit for the Allied war effort regardless. The Royal Air Force needed pilots to fly bomber aircraft, fighters, transports, as well as those who worked in a training capacity, and those who were in training or on the injured list. So not having to provide the hundreds of ferry pilots needed to move military aircraft all over the country and beyond, was a massive help to the nation's war effort.

Chapter One

Air Transport Auxiliary

The Air Transport Auxiliary (ATA) that was founded at the beginning of the Second World War was a civilian organization that was staffed by both men and women. These brave individuals made an enormous contribution to the Allied war effort by collecting new aircraft from the factories where they were made, or damaged and repaired aircraft to and from maintenance units, before flying them for the Royal Air Force and Royal Navy to military aerodromes and front-line squadrons all over the country and sometimes abroad, but not to aircraft carriers. They also flew service personnel on urgent duty from one place to another and performed work as air ambulance units.

In August 1939 the administration of the Air Transport Auxiliary was the responsibility of Gerard d'Erlanger, who was a director of British Airways Ltd, which was merged into the British Overseas Airways Corporation (BOAC) in 1940. Foreseeing the imminent outbreak of war in Europe, he had suggested a similar organization in a letter dated 24 May 1938.

On 10 October 1939 the Air Member for Supply and Organization (AMSO) took over from BOAC as the organization responsible for the administration of the Air Transport Auxiliary. The first pilots were assigned to the RAF Reserve Command and attached to RAF flights to ferry trainers, fighter and bomber aircraft from factories, maintenance units and storage to operational Royal Air Force stations. The Air Transport Auxiliary's Central Ferry Control, which allocated the required flights to all ferry pools, was based at RAF Andover.

The members of the Air Transport Auxiliary collected different nicknames throughout their years of existence, and one of them that stuck was 'Ancient and Tattered Airmen'. The first recruits came with a wide range of experience, but all had one thing in common; they were either too old or unfit for active military wartime service, some having previously served in the First World War. One man was even a retired admiral who wanted to do his bit. Then there were Charles Dutton and Stewart Keith-Jopp; both only had one arm. But despite their obvious handicaps this did not stop them from being able to fly such aircraft as the Spitfire and Typhoon.

After the war had started it was decided that a third ferry pool, one that was made up entirely of civilians should be set up at RAF White Waltham, near Maidenhead in Berkshire, and that began operating on 15 February 1940. On 22 July 1941 the Air Transport Auxiliary was placed under the control of Lord Beaverbrook's Ministry of Aircraft Production (MAP).

It was only after individuals had been turned down by the Royal Air Force or the Fleet Air Arm, for whatever reason, that they could be recruited by the Air Transport Auxiliary. This meant that women could apply. Age or disability were no barriers. The Second World War showed that in a crisis or a time of need anything was possible, hence how the Air Transport Auxiliary had members serving who had one leg, one arm, were short-sighted and one who only had one eye. If they could fly, they were welcome. Maybe this was a very early example of what diversity in the workplace looked like.

And being British wasn't a criterion for being recruited into the Air Transport Auxiliary. German nationals were not considered as suitable candidates, for obvious reasons, but pilots from twenty-eight different Allied or neutral countries were.

During its existence in the Second World War, the Air Transport Auxiliary had a total of 4,301 personnel who served with the organization across 16 locations. The breakdown of these members of staff was as follows: 2,786 ground staff, of whom 1,227 were engineers; male pilots accounted for a further 1,152 members of staff, followed by 168 female pilots, 151 flight engineers, 19 radio officers, and a combination of 27 Air Training Corps and Sea cadets.

From 1943 until the end of the war the women pilots who undertook this role were paid the same rate of pay as their male counterparts, which was a first for the British government.

By taking on this important role the men and women of the Air Transport Authority freed serving pilots who were urgently needed for front-line duties.

During the course of the war a total of 1,245 men and women from 25 different countries flew more than 147 different types of aircraft on 309,000 occasions, and did this without any radios, with no instrument-flying instruction, no machine guns to defend themselves if attacked by German aircraft and always at the mercy of the ever-changing British weather.

Of those 1,152 men and 168 women who flew for the Air Transport Authority, some 174 were killed whilst serving with the organization. This included 156 men and women who died as a result of being involved in fatal incidents.

Initially the idea was for the Air Transport Auxiliary to deliver mail, medical supplies, and military personnel to different locations the length and breadth of the country. No sooner had the war begun than the urgent need for aircraft being delivered to operational RAF stations and maintenance aerodromes was realised. If the responsibility for this was left down to the RAF, it would have placed a heavy burden upon it and greatly reduced its effectiveness. But in the early months of the war these duties did remain the responsibility of the RAF. It wasn't until the beginning of May 1940 that this changed. Initially the pilots of the Air Transport Auxiliary were given the task of transporting all military aircraft from the factories where they were made to RAF maintenance units to have machine guns and other such specialist equipment fitted to them. The following year, on 1 August 1941, the pilots of the Air Transport Auxiliary took over the role of the ferrying of RAF aircraft to operational RAF stations across the country. The main benefit of this change was that it freed the RAF pilots so that they were purely available for operational missions and training purposes.

At its peak the Air Transport Auxiliary had a total of fourteen ferry pools that stretched from Hamble, on the south coast of England, all the way up to Lossiemouth which is close to Inverness in Scotland.

With the end of the war the Air Transport Auxiliary, like many other wartime units, both those that had worked in a front-line capacity, and those in support roles, were suddenly surplus to requirements. The end for them came on 30 November 1945 at a ceremony held at what had been the Air Transport Auxiliary's Headquarters at RAF White Waltham. It was Lord Beaverbrook who gave a glowing but well-deserved tribute to those who had served with the Air Transport Auxiliary during the course of the war.

> Without the Air Transport Auxiliary, the days and nights of the Battle of Britain would have been conducted under conditions quite different from the actual events. They carried out the delivery of aircraft from the factories to the RAF, thus relieving countless numbers of RAF pilots for duty in the battle. Just as the Battle of Britain is the accomplishment and achievement of the RAF, likewise it can be declared that the Air Transport Auxiliary sustained and supported them in the battle. They were soldiers fighting in the struggle just as completely as if they had been engaged on the battlefront.

During the war members of the Air Transport Auxiliary flew a total of 415,000 hours and delivered more than 309,000 aircraft of 147 different types. These included Spitfires, Hurricanes, Mosquitoes, Mustangs, Lancasters, Halifaxes, Swordfish, Barracudas and Fortresses. Approximately 883 tons of freight were carried along with 3,430 passengers without any casualties; but 174 pilots, both men and women, were killed whilst serving with the Air Transport Auxiliary in the wartime years.

Initially, to comply with the Geneva Convention, and because many of the ferry pilots were nominally civilians, and/or women, aircraft were ferried with their fitted guns or other armament, unloaded. However, after encounters with German aircraft in which the ferried aircraft were unable to defend themselves, it was decided that all RAF aircraft that were flown by members of the Air Transport Auxiliary would be ferried with their guns fully armed.

Initially it was only men who were considered but needs often dictate the need for 'thinking outside the box', and so it was that a women's section of the Air Transport Auxiliary was organised under the command of Pauline Gower MBE on 14 November 1939.

On 1 January 1940 the first eight women pilots were accepted into service and were allowed to fly de Havilland Tiger Moth aircraft from their base in Hatfield. Those ground-breaking eight women were: Joan Hughes; Margaret Cunnison; Mona Friedlander; Rosemary Rees; Marion Wilberforce; Margaret Fairweather; Gabrielle Patterson; and Winifred Crossley Fair.

Joan Hughes, or, to give her full name, Joan Lily Amelia Hughes, was born in West Ham on 27 April 1918 and went on to become one of Britain's first female test pilots.

She started learning to fly in 1933, when she was just 15 years of age, at a time when there were no restrictions on how old someone had to be before they could take flying lessons. Within two years she had qualified as a pilot and, in doing so, had become Britain's youngest ever female pilot.

When she was accepted as an Air Transport Auxiliary pilot on 1 January 1940, she also became the youngest female pilot to join the service. Initially, like all her female colleagues, she was only allowed to fly Tiger Moth aircraft from their base at Hatfield aerodrome but in no time at all had racked up some 600 hours flying time, flying military aircraft around the country. Joan Hughes was a great example of how size and strength didn't always go hand in hand. Despite the fact that she was considerably small in stature, only 5 feet 2 inches tall, she went on to fly four-engined heavy bomber aircraft. Later in the war she became a senior pilot and the only female who qualified as an instructor on all types of British military aircraft that were in service at the time.

In 1946, with the war over, Joan was appointed MBE for her wartime service. She continued to work as a flying instructor for the Airways Aero Association at White Waltham and Booker airfields. She went on to appear in such films as *Those Magnificent Men in their Flying Machines* in 1965, *The Blue Max* in 1966 and *Thunderbird 6* in 1968. She flew her last flight in 1985 at the age of 67, having clocked up 11,800 hours in her flying logbook. She died in Somerset on 16 August 1993, aged 75.

Margaret Cunnison was already a highly respected flying instructor before the outbreak of war and went on to fulfil the same role with the Air Transport Auxiliary, where she was their chief instructor at Hatfield, tasked with evaluating and training new pilots. In 1943 she quit her position with the Air Transport Auxiliary to get married.

Mona Friedlander was another who had been a pilot before the war and who saw enlisting in the Air Transport Auxiliary as her way of doing her bit for the war effort. She also had a navigator's licence, just to add to her usefulness in the air. She continued in her role until 1943 when she left to get married.

Rosemary Rees had also been a pilot before the war and had held an instructor's licence since 1938, the same year that she decided to fly to Germany in her Miles Hawk to attend an air show. With the war imminent, she left in time and returned to England, enlisting in the Air Transport Auxiliary, where she went on to become second in command at the Hamble Ferry Pool in Hampshire. After the war she continued to enjoy her love of flying and set up an air taxi service. She died in 1994, aged 92.

Marion Wilberforce was born on 22 July 1902, one of seven children to John and Anne Ogilvie, her father being the 9th Laird of Boyndlie. As a 12-year-old child she had to suddenly grow up very quickly indeed: when her father lost all interest in running the family home and estate, it was Marion who took over, and she could often be seen riding on horseback to collect the rents from the estate's tenants.

After being educated at home by a number of French governesses, when she was 17 years of age in 1919 she was sent to the Convent of Jesus and Mary at Stony Stratford in Buckinghamshire. There she remained until 1921. In 1922 she continued her education at Somerville College Oxford where she read for a degree in agriculture. Whilst at Oxford she played an active part in university life, was a member of the university's women's mountaineering team and also obtained a certificate of merit in the form of martial arts known as Ju-Jitsu.

Her love for flying, it would be fair to say, came from two of her elder brothers who were both aviators. Having seen them become pilots, she became hooked on the idea of following in their footsteps and qualifying as a pilot. She got herself a job and saved hard and fast until she had enough money to begin taking flying lessons. Marion obtained her private pilot's licence in 1930 and, seven years later, had enough money to purchase her own de Havilland Cirrus Moth, mainly from funds she had made on the stock exchange as a child, having been taught how to invest by her uncle, Reginald Prendergast.

She later changed this to a Hornet Moth aircraft for tax purposes as those were classified as farm implements and kept in a barn. They were used to ferry poultry about, as well as Dexter cattle which she bred at Nevendon Manor in Essex, precisely because they could fit into aeroplanes. On one occasion she flew a calf back from Hungary.

In 1929 the City of Bristol Corporation purchased 298 acres of farmland to the south of the city, near Whitchurch, to build a new municipal airport which duly opened for business on 31 May 1930. It was such a prestigious occasion that the opening was officially conducted by His Royal Highness Prince George, Duke of Kent. The Bristol and Wessex Aerodrome Club, who had been asked by the government to assist in the training of new pilots, relocated to the newly opened airport and, together with Bristol Corporation, managed the facilities. The first buildings were a hangar and a clubhouse for the flying club. Nice to see that they got their priorities right.

In July 1938, with the threat of war never too far away, the British government formed a Civil Air Guard. Men who had signed up to become part of the Royal Air Force Volunteer Reserve found themselves at Whitchurch aerodrome in Bristol to undergo their training with No. 33 Elementary and Reserve Flying Training School.

In September 1939 Whitchurch was requisitioned by the Air Ministry and declared a restricted area. Because of the threat to London and its surrounding areas from German bombing raids, British Airways Ltd, along with Imperial Airways, moved from their previous bases at Croydon Airport and Heston Aerodrome respectively and relocated to Whitchurch Airport. This meant that nearly an additional sixty aircraft had descended on Whitchurch.

The government's National Air Communications, which had been formed to oversee wartime air transport movements, became part of the new community that had become connected with Whitchurch. A new tarmac runway was added, along with sufficient taxiways to make the airport fully effective.

Security was increased greatly to meet all the extra demands that had been thrust upon the still relatively new airport. Suddenly the camp at Whitchurch wasn't so inviting anymore, with guard towers, armed sentries and barbed wire topping off the entire perimeter fence.

At the outbreak of the Second World War *Pauline Mary de Peauly Gower Fahie*, already a qualified pilot and writer, established the women's branch of the Air Transport Auxiliary. Born in Tonbridge, Kent, on 22 July 1910, she was the daughter of Sir Robert Vaughan Power, a solicitor and the Conservative Member of Parliament for Hackney Central, a seat won at the 1924 general election. In the 1929 general election he did not contest the Hackney seat, but instead was elected as MP for Gillingham in Kent.

Pauline was educated at the Beechwood Sacred Heart School in Tunbridge Wells. It was in her late teens that she first became infatuated with flying; she had her first flying experience alongside Alan Cobham, later to be Sir Alan Cobham, First World War veteran of the Royal Flying Corps, and a post-war pioneer of long-distance aviation.

In 1931, along with fellow female aviator Dorothy Spicer, Gower began an air-taxi service in Kent. Spicer held an A pilot's licence, which allowed her to fly, and was also qualified as a ground engineer, whilst Gower held a B pilot's licence which allowed her to carry fare-paying passengers. They purchased a Gypsy Moth between them for the business, but it became increasingly difficult for them to even cover their running costs, let alone make a worthwhile profit.

Throughout the 1930s, during a period that was both progressive and exciting in the world of aviation, Gower continued her flying, taking part in numerous air displays all over the country. This was also a time where she developed her writing which included both poetry and stories for established journals.

In 1936 the Air Ministry awarded her a second-class navigator's licence, making her the first British woman to achieve such a distinction and, in London in 1938, she became a civil defence commissioner with the Civil Air Guard, a scheme subsidised by the British government that helped pay the costs of flying lessons for members of affiliated flying clubs in return for a future commitment to military service.

With the outbreak of the Second World War, Gower saw her chance to do her bit for the nation's war effort and came up with the idea to form a women's section of the newly-formed Air Transport Auxiliary, which initially had only been for men.

On 16 December 1939 the first group of twelve potential women pilots of the Air Transport Auxiliary assembled at Whitchurch in Bristol and were flight-tested in a Gypsy Moth. From this group of twelve women, eight were selected and given the rank of second officer.

Marion Wilberforce was one of the eight who passed. When she joined the Air Transport Auxiliary she was already an extremely experienced pilot, having racked up a staggering 900 flying hours. By March 1943 this had more than tripled to 2,700.

During 1940 the Air Transport Auxiliary, had established No. 2 Ferry Pilots Pool at Whitchurch. The aircraft that the pilots there flew included Blenheims, Beaufighters and Beauforts that had been built at Filton in Gloucestershire, Hurricanes, built by the Gloster Aircraft Company at Brockworth, Gloucestershire, and Whirlwinds and Spitfires produced by Westland Aircraft Company of Yeovil in Somerset.

Having flown Spitfires, Hurricanes and Lancaster bombers, to name but a few, Marion Wilberforce went on to become deputy commander of No. 5 Ferry Pool at Hatfield and the commander of No. 12 Ferry Pool at Cosford, making her one of only two women who held such a position in the Air Transport Auxiliary.

On one occasion she arrived at a factory where she had gone to collect an aircraft only to discover that the employees had all gone on strike and that the aircraft she had been sent to collect could not be released. On hearing this news, she marched off purposefully to the canteen, climbed on a table and gave a resounding speech about the war effort on the home front and the importance of everybody doing their bit. This secured the release of the aircraft she had come to collect.

The early female members of the Air Transport Auxiliary were met initially with prejudice from their male colleagues, both those with whom they worked and those in overall command. This resulted in the female pilots initially only being allowed to fly non-operational aircraft but, by mid-1941, Marion Wilberforce was flying operational machines including Hurricanes and Spitfires which she piloted as a matter of course. This did not go down at all well with her male colleagues, who saw their female counterparts as being beneath them, which they must definitely were not.

The first Spitfire Marion flew was donated by the citizens of Grimsby and accordingly called 'Grimsby II'. During 1942 she mastered the entire range of twin-engined medium bombers, including the Wellington and Mosquito. Two years later she became one of only eleven women pilots trained to fly four-engined bombers such as the Lancaster. By the end of the war she had flown most, if not all, of the aircraft flown by members of the Air Transport Authority. In the early days she had also had to fly civilian aircraft that had been impressed, including her own Hornet Moth which was later lost on a reconnaissance flight.

Women pilots were not allowed to fly Hurricane aircraft until 19 July 1941, nor Spitfires until August 1941. The reason behind this decision had nothing to do with the women's flying ability, but everything to do with arrogance and outdated socially held beliefs about women's place in society: flying aircraft was a man's job, and certainly not one that women should be doing. But, by their skill and ability, the women proved that they were just as good and able as their male counterparts to fly any and all types of aircraft.

Some days Marion would ferry as many as four different aircraft that were situated in different locations; between July and December 1944 she delivered 114 aircraft all over the country. At the war's end and by the time the Air Transport Auxiliary had been disbanded Marion had served with them for the entire five years of their existence.

After the war she was appointed MBE for her wartime contributions but politely declined the award. After the war she continued to fly but was obviously not a great one for unnecessary change as she did not have a radio set in her aircraft, until she was forced to by law. When she wanted to land, she would circle the airfield, dipping and re-dipping her wings, and then wait until somebody appeared on the runway waving a flag and indicating that it was safe enough for her to land.

She navigated by following features on the ground and if she lost her way she would simply land at a convenient location, climb out of her aircraft and either find someone to ask for directions or find a signpost so that she could work out the direction in which she had to travel. But despite not wanting to have a radio onboard her aircraft, she was very safety conscious, even carrying a rubber dinghy in case she went down over water.

Nothing seemed to faze her. In 1949 she flew to Helsinki in Finland en route to paying a visit to her brother Neil, an air attaché at the British embassy in Moscow. Flying to her was the equivalent of somebody going for a drive today. She would regularly get in her aircraft and fly off to wherever took her fancy, usually to visit friends, sometimes even taking in trips across the English Channel to visit somewhere of her choice in Europe. She was even known to have taken off from her home in Wickford, fly to Luxembourg, have lunch, and return home afterwards.

On one occasion she was a tad fortunate to return home at all. In 1953 she had been on a visit to friends in Austria, when she inadvertently flew into Russian airspace and was fired upon.

She was 80 years of age when she finally decided to give up her beloved flying, something which she had done and enjoyed for some sixty years. She was wealthy enough to be able to afford to own her own aircraft. The last aircraft she owned was a Tiger Moth, which she sold to an Australian sheep farmer.

It would be fair to describe her as being somewhat of a maverick when it came to flying and, as a post-war civilian pilot, she often did not do as she was supposed to which today would no doubt have seen her lose her coveted flying licence.

She married Robert Wilberforce in 1932 who had been torn between a feeling that he had a vocation for the priesthood and the possibility of getting married. To try to resolve his uncertainty he spent six months living in Ampleforth Abbey in North Yorkshire. When the six months was up, Marion was waiting outside the gates, keenly awaiting his decision. He decided on a life of marriage and returned to their home at Nevendon Manor in Wickford, where they farmed chickens, pigs and Dexter cattle, still using her aircraft to convey her animals about rather than vehicular transport.

She died in July 1996, when she was 93 years of age.

Margaret Fairweather was born on 23 September 1901 at West Denton Hall, near Newcastle-upon-Tyne. As a member of the Air Transport Auxiliary she flew numerous different aircraft during her wartime military service, including Tiger Moths and Hurricanes. She was also the first woman to fly a single-seat Supermarine Spitfire.

Prior to the war she had been an instructor with the Civil Air Guard, part of a scheme set up by the British government in 1938 whereby they subsidised the cost of pilot training for members of flying clubs in return for agreeing to become military pilots in a time of war; in essence that meant becoming a member of the Royal Air Force Volunteer Reserve.

She died on 4 August 1944, of an extensive skull fracture, when the aircraft she was flying crashed as a result of what turned out to be mechanical problems with the fuel tank. Her sister Kitty, who was also onboard, survived the crash but was injured.

Margaret had lost her husband, who was also a pilot with the Air Transport Auxiliary, just four months before her death when he, too, died in a plane crash whilst flying for the Air Transport Auxiliary on 3 April 1944. Margaret is buried in Dunure Cemetery, South Ayrshire.

Gabrielle Patterson became the first woman in Britain to qualify as a flying instructor in 1935 and went on to become the chief instructor of the Civil Air Guard in Essex.

Winifred Crossley Fair had been a pilot before the war and had spent much of her time working as a stunt pilot in an air circus and towing advertising banners behind her aircraft. She enlisted in the Air Transport Auxiliary in 1940 and went on to serve with them throughout the war until it was disbanded in November 1945. In her personal life she married Captain Peter Fair who was the head of BOAC airlines.

These eight ladies were the first of 166 female pilots who flew for the Air Transport Auxiliary during the course of the Second World War, fifteen of whom lost their lives in service. The female members of the Air Transport Auxiliary acquired the nickname of 'Attagirls', as well as a high profile amongst elements of the national press because of the uniqueness of their situation.

It wasn't just British women who volunteered to serve with the Air Transport Auxiliary; they came from far and wide to do their bit for the Allied war effort. They volunteered from Australia, Canada, New Zealand, South Africa, the United States, Holland, Poland, Argentina and Chile. In total, during the course of the war, 166 female pilots served with the Air Transport Auxiliary which was one in eight of its entire complement of pilots.

A notable member of the Air Transport Auxiliary was American pilot Jaqueline Cochran who returned to the United States and began a similar organization there, which she entitled the Women Airforce Service Pilots, or WASP. Cochran is a very interesting and important figure in the history of female aviation. She set many land marks for women pilots. She was the first woman to fly a four-engine bomber across the Atlantic and went on to become a lieutenant colonel in the USAF Reserve. She was a female world speed record holder and an advocate for training women as astronauts in the early stages of the space programme. She also broke the sound barrier on 18 May 1953 and was a prominent racing pilot. In 1943 she wrote a letter to Lieutenant Colonel Robert Olds suggesting that women pilots be employed to fly non-combat missions.

The American women pilots were not paid anywhere near as much as their male counterparts. They received as little as 65 per cent of the pay given to their male colleagues.

The initial training for Air Transport Auxiliary personnel was carried out at the RAF's Central Flying School but it wasn't long before the Air Transport Auxiliary had developed their own pilot training programme. All their pilots began by qualifying to fly light, single-engine aircraft and only when it was believed that they had made steady progress were they allowed to continue on to flying bigger and heavier aircraft. They basically gained their experience by ferrying their aircraft around the country to different locations. But after they had proved that they were more than capable pilots they couldn't just be given different aircraft to fly; instead they returned to training school to qualify to fly the next type of aircraft. It was felt to be a better way for pilots to learn, i.e. at their own pace, rather than trying to keep up to a rigid timetable that didn't have any flexibility built into it.

The training allowed for a pilot who had qualified in flying a particular type of aircraft to fly other aircraft in the same class, even if they had never trained or even seen that aircraft before. To assist pilots to be able to do this each of them was provided with *Ferry Pilot Notes*, a two-ringed, blue-covered booklet, which comprised a number of cards that included critical information for each of the aircraft a pilot might be requested to fly.

A pilot who was qualified to fly, say, a four-engined bomber could still be asked to fly a single-seater aircraft if circumstances dictated the need for them to do so, even if they were not happy about being asked.

Pilots who flew for the Air Transport Auxiliary were not trained to the same level as an RAF pilot, as there was simply no need to do so. Their job was to simply collect an aircraft from point A and fly it to point B without taking any unnecessary risks; that was it. They did not have to know anything about aerobatics, defensive tactics, attacking an enemy from above or how to dive-bomb an enemy position.

As with all such organizations, and despite it being a civilian one, the Air Transport Auxiliary had a rank structure that was based loosely on that of officers serving in the RAF.

Senior Commander – designated by four broad yellow hoops on the cuffs of each sleeve of the pilot's tunic.

Flight Captain – designated by two outer broad yellow hoops on the cuff of each sleeve of the pilot's tunic and a narrow central one.

First Officer – designated by two broad yellow hoops on the cuff of each sleeve of the pilot's tunic.

Second Officer – designated by one broad and one narrow yellow hoop on the cuff of each sleeve of the pilot's tunic.

Third Officer – designated by one broad yellow hoop on the cuff of each sleeve of the pilot's tunic.

The following is a list of the different ferry pools that were situated around the country and helped the Air Transport Auxiliary not only cover the entire country but cut down the time it would take them to deliver much needed aircraft to operational flying stations.

No. 1 Ferry Pool Air Transport Auxiliary, White Waltham, Maidenhead.

No. 2 Ferry Pool Air Transport Auxiliary, Whitchurch, Bristol.

No. 3 Ferry Pool Air Transport Auxiliary, Harwarden, Chester.

No. 4 Ferry Pool Air Transport Auxiliary, Prestwick, Ayrshire.

No. 5 Ferry Pool Air Transport Auxiliary, Thame, Oxfordshire. (Training Unit).

No. 6 Ferry Pool Air Transport Auxiliary, Ratcliffe, Leicester.

No. 7 Ferry Pool Air Transport Auxiliary, Sherburn-in-Elmet, Leeds.

No. 8 Ferry Pool Air Transport Auxiliary, Sydenham, Belfast.

No. 9 Ferry Pool Air Transport Auxiliary, Aston Down, Gloucestershire.

No. 10 Ferry Pool Air Transport Auxiliary, Lossiemouth, Moray.

No. 12 Ferry Pool Air Transport Auxiliary, Cosford, Staffordshire.

No. 14 Ferry Pilot Pool Air Transport Auxiliary, Ringway, Manchester.
No. 15 Ferry Pool Air Transport Auxiliary, Hamble, Southampton.
No. 16 Ferry Pool Air Transport Auxiliary, Kirkbride, Carlisle.
Initial Flying Training School Air Training Auxiliary.
Air Movements Flight Air Transport Auxiliary, 1942-45.
Advanced Flying Training School Air Transport Auxiliary, 1942-45.

As for Pauline Gower she was appointed MBE in 1942 for her services to aviation. In 1945 she married Wing Commander Bill Fahie but sadly theirs was destined to be a short marriage; she died at just 36 years of age on 2 March 1947 whilst giving birth to her twin sons who both survived.

It wasn't just pilots that the Air Transport Auxiliary required. They also required flight engineers who, in some respects, were just as important as the pilots when it came to moving the bigger aircraft, such as the four-engined Catalina and Sunderland flying boats, along with Dakota aircraft between their pick-up and drop-off points. One such member of the Air Transport Auxiliary, and one of its flight engineers at White Waltham, was Freddie Laker, later to become Sir Freddie Laker, king of the cheap flights across the Atlantic with Laker Airlines.

Another member of the Air Transport Auxiliary, John Gulson, was awarded the George Medal for his bravery in rescuing the crew of a Halifax bomber which had crash-landed at White Waltham in July 1944; it smashed into the railway with live bombs onboard.

Four women served as flight engineers with the Air Transport Auxiliary. One of them, Janice Harrington, was too short to be a pilot and so became a flight engineer instead. She was killed in a Mosquito accident in March 1944 and was buried in a Maidenhead cemetery.

Chapter Two

Newspaper Coverage

This chapter looks at the Air Transport Auxiliary and the men and women who served in it through the eyes of the Press. I have sifted through a number of national and local British newspapers looking for related stories that were anything to do with the service, good, bad or indifferent. Some of the following articles are detailed accounts of some of the accidents in which ferry pilots were involved, many of which were fatal for the pilots concerned.

Some of these stories look at those who were killed in car crashes. There is an account of one individual who killed another man, the result of a car crash, was sent to prison as a punishment, and still went on to become a pilot with the Air Transport Auxiliary.

Each of the articles have one thing in common: they are all about young men and women who came to the aid of the British nation throughout the years of the Second World War in an effort to help defeat Nazi Germany and her allies. Thankfully for the democratic countries of the free world, their efforts played a part in ensuring that Nazi Germany was eventually forced into having to concede to an unconditional surrender, and an end to the madness they had put in place throughout Europe.

This article appeared on page 4 of the well-known national newspaper, the *Sunday Mirror*, on Sunday 3 December 1939, under the headline, 'MP's Flying Daughter will lead Eves of RAF.'

> Key job for Britain's women pilots has been secured by the twenty-seven-year-old daughter of Sir Robert Gower, MP for Gillingham, Kent.

Pauline Gower is to lead Britain's new air squadron, the women's pilot section of the Air Transport Auxiliary.

Her colleagues will make history in the great story of British aviation, women will pilot RAF planes from the manufacturers to the flying schools and reserve centres.

They will pilot light machines at first, but later on may be called on to handle bombers and 350 mph fighters.

Hitherto no woman has ever so much as been allowed to enter a military aircraft as a passenger. Even the wife of the Air Minister is not allowed to fly in Air Force machines.

The Air Transport Auxiliary has been formed from the ranks of veteran pilots whose fighting days are over. They are mostly the 'over forty-fives', with anything up to 10,000 hours experience as commercial pilots. They ferry bombers, fighters and other aircraft between manufacturers and the squadrons.

Britain's 'Eves of the RAF' are chosen from seasoned women pilots who have 1,000 hours of solo flying to their credit.

They will have to face some 'sticky' flying. There will be no wireless in their planes and they will have to fly in all weathers.

Miss Gower is now recruiting the women pilots who will be first to 'take off'.

She is the only girl in the British Empire to hold 'A' and 'B' flying licences. She has the second-class navigator's ticket, a blind-flying certificate and the GPO wireless licence and parachute licence.

From 1930 to 1939 Miss Gower gave 'joy rides' in her plane to more than 20,000 people in this country, without an accident.

When reading through the previous article it is clear to see that Miss Gower was most definitely the best qualified person for the job, with a combination of hands-on experience coupled with a credibility that would have both impressed and been respected by those under her command and direction.

The following article appeared in the *Kent & Sussex Courier* newspaper dated Friday 15 December 1939, concerning the use of women as ferry pilots for the Air Transport Auxiliary.

> Under a scheme launched by the Air Ministry, women pilots will be employed to ferry new RAF aircraft of light training types from the factory where they are made to an aerodrome for storage until they are required for service purposes. To begin with it is contemplated that only eight women pilots will be employed. They will form a section of Air Transport Auxiliary Service under British Airways Limited. Miss Pauline Gower has been appointed to take administrative charge of the section.

Although it isn't mentioned in the article, it was Miss Gower's idea in the first place to have such a section as part of the Air Transport Auxiliary. It also undoubtedly helped that her father, Sir Robert Gower, was a Member of Parliament at the time and would have no doubt been able to use his influence, such as it was, to greatly assist his daughter's idea.

As the eight selected women commenced their training with the Air Transport Auxiliary, local and national newspapers were full of articles and photographs about them and the journey they were about to begin.

The *Derby Daily Telegraph* for Wednesday 10 January 1940 included the following article.

Air work by Women

RAF Ferry Service

> Women pilots well known in civil aviation before the war, today began their new 'ferry' service by flying aeroplanes direct from an aerodrome adjoining a factory somewhere in England to a Royal Air Force station.

They form a section of the Air transport Auxiliary. The service is being organised by British Airways under the Air Ministry.

So far eight women have been selected, Mrs Winifred Crossley, Miss M. Cunnison, the Hon. Mrs Fairweather, Miss Mona Friedlander, Miss Joan Hughes, Mrs G. Patterson, Mrs Rosemary Rees, and Mrs Marion Wilberforce. They are under the direction of Miss Pauline Gower, daughter of Sir Robert Gower MP.

It is expected that the number will be increased shortly. Each of the successful candidates has had several years of flying experience, and most of them can claim more than 1,000 flying hours. They are given salaries with flight pay.

Except for the colour, which is dark blue, the uniforms of the women pilots resemble those of officers in the RAF, and they wear navy blue forage caps.

An interesting aspect of the newly selected female members of the Air Transport Auxiliary, which had not been discussed in the press up to that time, was the women's wages. An article that appeared on Monday 22 January 1940, in the *Lancashire Evening Post*, changed all that.

Women Air Pilots get £6 a Week

They pay for their own Billets

The nine women pilots of the Air Transport Auxiliary get about £6 a week, not £600 a year as had been previously reported. Out of that they have to pay for their billets, their blue shirts, black shoes and stockings.

There is a waiting list of 30 women pilots for the service. The fact that the pay is lower than was at first reported does not settle, however, a controversy among men pilots. The men complaining are mostly civil pilots, and they ask why women were engaged on behalf of the Air Ministry when there exist scores of efficient men pilots over 30.

Those who devised the scheme point out that the women release men pilots for ferrying front-line warplanes, to which civil pilots reply, 'the women pilots are ferrying elementary trainers. Is it suggested that the men with licences, who have several hundred hours flying, are less efficient?'

A theory that is given considerable weight in some quarters is that the introduction of women into this ancillary of the RAF, which is intended to be extended, is a preparation for the time when there may be a shortage of men pilots.

The minimum requirements of the women pilots before acceptance in the Air Transport Auxiliary was that they should have had 250 hours flying. They also had to undergo a flying test. None of them was found to have had less than 600 hours, and some had up to 2,000 hours.

All had the commercial, or 'B' licences, or else the more junior 'A' licence, endorsed for instructing. Some had been flying regularly since 1930.

The discussion about women pilots was, I believe, nothing more sinister than about the period of time we are talking about. It has to be remembered that in the 1930s, and in the following decades all the way through until definitely the 1970s, women in the workplace were somewhat restricted in both the roles they undertook and the wages which they earned for their toils. There were even more questions when the woman in question was married. In such a case a woman was expected to stay at home, have children and look after the family, whilst the man went out to work. There were cases where it was not socially acceptable for a man having his wife out working, it was actually seen as a slight on a man's character if he could not provide for his family. There was also the other consideration of wages and the higher amount that would be paid to a man for doing the exact same job as a woman. Was it a case of trying to get the work done more cheaply? If this was the case originally, all that changed when women pilots were paid the same as men from 1943 onwards.

Things didn't always run smoothly for the Air Transport Auxiliary, for numerous different reasons. This brief article from the *Portsmouth Evening News* dated Tuesday 6 February 1940 was an example of a somewhat unexpected nature.

A warrant for the arrest of Percy Randall, of the Plaza Garage, Britannia Road, Portsmouth, and at present serving in the Air Transport Auxiliary, was issued this morning after he had failed to appear in the Second Court to answer a summons for assault.

Exactly one week later, on Tuesday 13 February 1940, Percy Randall appeared at Portsmouth police court. In that day's edition of the *Portsmouth Evening News* an article appeared on the back page which covered Randall's court appearance.

Struck Bank Official
'Cowardly Assault'
Man Lost His Temper
Fined £5

What was described as a cowardly and unprovoked assault was described at Portsmouth Police Court, today, when Percy Randall of 21 Britannia Road North, Southsea, managing director of the Plaza Garage, was fined £5 with £5. 5s costs for assaulting Henry Gordon Gibbs of Clarendon Road, Southsea, an accountant in the employ of the National Provincial Bank, Commercial Road, Portsmouth.

Mr Glanville, for the prosecution, outlining the case, explained that there had been certain negotiations between the bank and the garage extending over a long period, as a result of which it had been necessary for the bank to take a check of the stock in the garage.

On January 9, an appointment had been made for Gibbs to attend at the garage to make the customary check. He went there with another official of the bank.

Randall started a conversation, but suddenly lost his temper and used disgusting language and made unpleasant and filthy remarks about the bank, the manager and Gibbs.

He picked up Gibbs's papers and rammed them into the complainant's face, following this with several severe blows, one of which fractured Gibbs's nose.

Gibbs gave evidence supporting Mr Granville's statement and in cross examination said that immediately war broke out proceedings were taken in Chancery concerning debentures.

Randall, in the witness box, said it was really on the suggestion of Gibbs and his manager that he took up the loan, and when he spoke to Gibbs on January 9 he told him he thought the bank had treated him harshly in the matter, referring to the fact that they had made several attempts to get a receiver appointed after recalling the debentures.

When he went to the garage he thought Gibbs had been there long enough and ordered him off his premises. He refused and there was a struggle.

No more than two blows were struck, and they were during the struggle.

Mr King said that three times the bank had been to Mr Justice Bennett asking for a receiver to be appointed, and this would have meant selling up the business.

Randall was naturally sore and the bank also, and they were working at strained relations.

After the Magistrates had retired, the Lord Mayor, Councillor D.L. Daley, said that he and his fellow magistrates had considered it a cowardly and unprovoked assault. They had considered whether to send Randall to prison.

Although not mentioned in the article, the fact that he was a serving captain in the Air Transport Auxiliary must have helped him greatly, and was quite possibly the main reason why he did not receive a custodial sentence.

Randall's story highlights a good point. Now I would not start by referring to him as part of the collective 'the common man' as, being a person who was able to engage in flying as a pastime, suggests a certain degree of affluence and wealth, but he would, I suggest, come in to the category of being 'just a normal person'. With the outbreak of war, he could have just 'kept his head down' and carried on with his business as he would likely have been too old for military service but he didn't do that. Like lots of British people he wanted to do his bit for his country in its time of need and, by signing up with the Air Transport Auxiliary, he certainly did do his bit. Randall and his colleagues were flying military aircraft all over the country and sometimes across the English Channel. They had no radio communications in case of emergency, no machine guns to defend themselves with if engaged by enemy aircraft and, for most of them, no previous aerial combat experience or training, which would at least provide them with an opportunity for making good their escape. The men and women of the Air Transport Auxiliary were undoubtedly very brave individuals.

The following story is about Percy Randall who held the rank of captain in the Air Transport Auxiliary. At just after 1 o'clock in the afternoon on Monday 17 March 1941 Randall took off from Luton on a ferry flight to White Waltham, near Maidenhead in Berkshire, in a brand-new Hawker Hurricane 1 aircraft, serial number Z7010. But, after having been in the air for just fifteen minutes, Randall's Hurricane crashed at Holly Green, near Princes Risborough.

Randall's 'service record' showed that he held an 'A' licence and was a reliable and exceptionally capable pilot who had over 550 hours of flying experience, more than twenty of which had been spent flying

Hurricanes, and that he had flown twenty-six different types of aircraft whilst serving with the Air Transport Auxiliary.

Records show that, at the time of the crash, weather conditions were not particularly ideal for flying with rain, fog and clouds all apparent in the area. Randall had in fact collected the aircraft from Henlow the previous evening but, because of inclement weather, had been unable to land at his intended location and instead had diverted to Luton where he had spent the night. Things hadn't improved that much by the following morning and, as the weather was still bad at White Waltham, he had been advised to wait it out at Luton until the weather had improved.

Just after lunch on the day of the crash, Randall took the decision to take off from Luton and make his way to White Waltham even though the weather there meant landing would have been far from straightforward.

In relation to the crash, it is believed that the aircraft stalled before going into a spin, and that all that is known for sure is that Randall's Hurricane struck the ground at a steep angle and at high speed; his body had been thrown from the cockpit of the aircraft and was discovered a short distance away.

A subsequent investigation into the crash, carried out by members of the Air Ministry's Accidents Investigations Branch, noted that in their opinion, because of the weather conditions which prevailed at the time Randall should not have taken off from Luton.

On the website, www.aircrewremembered.com, there is a group photograph of Randall and eleven other members of the Air Transport Auxiliary. It is not clear when the photograph was taken but it was sometime during the course of the Second World War. By the end of the war six of those in the photograph, including Randall, had been killed. The others were Walter Handley, James Watson, Donald Kennard, Robert Sandeman and Walter Mason.

Wednesday 5 June 1940 saw an article appear in the *Lancashire Evening Post* about a female member of the Air Transport Auxiliary who in essence had been forced to resign. The reason behind the resignation, it could be said, was somewhat unique.

Woman Pilot Resigns

Lady Bailey, wife of Sir Abe Bailey, has left the women pilots' section of the Air Transport Auxiliary, for which she was flying aircraft from the factories to the RAF squadrons.

Her resignation, I understand, arises not from her own choice but from certain criticisms of her appointment in view of her wealth and other considerations.

The women pilots receive £6 a week. Lady Bailey learned to fly when she was nearly 40, and has made a number of long flights and, although 50 years old this year, is still an excellent pilot.

She is now seeking some alternative use for her vigorous and energetic talents. At present she is organising local defence volunteers at her home in Oxfordshire.

How strange to hear of someone having to give up such a worthwhile job, and one of such national importance, because she was a wealthy woman. It had only been announced in March 1940 that Lady Bailey, and Mrs Lois Butler, the wife of Mr Alan Butler, chairman of the de Havilland Aircraft Company, had both joined other women pilots in the Air Transport Auxiliary.

The Honourable Mary Westenra was born in Rossmore Castle, County Monaghan, Ireland, on 1 December 1890. She was a relatively late beginner when it came to flying, not obtaining her pilot's licence until 1927 when she was 37 years of age. Having acquired her right to fly, she did not waste any time, and, within a matter of months, she became the first woman to fly across the Irish Sea. On 5 July 1927, whilst flying a de Havilland DH.60 Cirrus II Moth, she set a world height record for a light aircraft, reaching a height of 17,283 feet. She continued to be a prestigious flyer throughout the 1920s and 1930s. It is believed that, in February 1931, she became the first woman to take aerial photographs as part of the Kharga Oasis archaeological project in Egypt.

During the Second World War she became a section officer in the Women's Auxiliary Air Force.

She married Sir Abraham (Abe) Bailey on 5 September 1911, and they went on to have five children, the last of whom was born in 1921. Mary died in Cape Town, South Africa, on 29 July 1960 when she was 69 years of age.

The *Liverpool Echo* from Saturday 13 July 1940 included an article about the death of a female pilot.

Wirral Woman Pilot's Death

When on Active Service

It is announced today that the well-known Merseyside airwoman, Mrs Elsie Joy Davison, has died following a flying accident when on active service. She is believed to be the first woman pilot to have died on active service.

Mrs Davison was killed at an RAF flying school where she was attending a refresher course prior to taking up piloting work with the Air Transport Auxiliary, civil flyers who 'ferry' new planes from factories to RAF stations.

An RAF sergeant instructor who was in the plane with her was also killed. It was only recently that she had volunteered to become an Air Transport Auxiliary pilot, together with Amy Johnson and other recruits, many of whom had to take refresher courses before being allowed to start Air Transport Auxiliary work.

Mrs Davison, aged about 30, was a well-known figure in aviation circles on Merseyside, where for many years she was engaged in an airways business with her husband. When they started an air service from Liverpool Airport to North Wales resorts in 1937, she often piloted airliners herself. She was also a member of Liverpool Aero Club.

She gained her first experience as an airwoman in Canada, but was living in Chester when she married Mr W. Frank Davison, of Woodford and Ellesmere Port, a prominent local aviator, seven years ago. They carried on a business as Utility Airways Ltd, from the Hooten and Little Sutton districts. At one time Mrs Davison was the only woman apart from Amy Johnson, holding a pilot's licence, and also a ground engineer's certificate.

In 1935 she 'vanished' from the sky during the night when assisting Merseyside Territorial anti-aircraft units to practice 'spotting' by searchlight.

Time and time again she cleverly eluded the searchlights, but when it was found she had gone altogether some anxiety was felt.

Her brother, Mr Frederick Alan Irving Muntz, is chairman of Heston Flying Club and one of the leading figures in commercial air circles at home, and in Egypt and India.

Saturday 31 August 1940 saw an article about Captain Norman Edgar appear in the *Lancashire Evening Post*, describing his position in the Air Transport Auxiliary.

Captain Norman Edgar, short, genial, middle-aged, erstwhile managing director and founder of Western Airways, is doing a war job after his own heart.

Surrounded by metal graphs, weather and flying maps, he pulls a microphone across his desk each morning and speaks into it the names of the pilots who are serving the RAF with new and repaired fighters, bombers and reconnaissance machines, the type they are to fly that day, and their destination.

His job, he says, is to 'marry aircraft'.

By this Captain Edgar means that across the intricate network of factories, airfields, balloon barrages, sudden bad weather, enemy air attacks, he has to guide his men and their machines so that each arrives at the proper destination at the proper time.

Sometimes pilots who have flown a new machine from factory to airfield, have to take a damaged aircraft from the same airfield for full repair at some other point.

Captain Edgar's organization is the Air Transport Auxiliary, run by the British Airways.

He started the war in control of a handful of amateur pilots, for whose efforts he has high praise. Some of them were pilots in the last war who had not flown since 1918.

At first, I gather, amateurs and professionals were shy of each other. Now, I am told, they get along well together.

Captain Edgar likes to show the 'Berchtesgaden Belle' to his few official visitors. It is the chassis of an old lorry, brought for £10, with a body of armour plating, an aeroplane revolving turret, and a wicked-looking Vickers machine gun.

The 'belle' awaits any Junkers seeking to interrupt Captain Norman's work.

On Monday 16 September 1940 the *Daily Gazette for Middlesbrough* published a great article which showed the true spirit of these civilian 'Ferry Pilots'.

It told the story of one brave individual and just how far he was prepared to push himself in an effort to do his bit for the war effort. Each and every one of us possesses the ability to be brave, but very few of us ever have the need or the opportunity to display those inner qualities that sets us apart from our peers.

As if to add even more intrigue to this man's story, he wasn't named, almost making him a Scarlet Pimpernel type character. Flying any type of aircraft, whether four-engine bomber or high-speed fighter aircraft, was no easy feat and required skill, nerves of steel, composure, calmness under pressure and, of course, the mandatory two hands. Not this guy.

Just to make things even more complicated, he flew aircraft for the Air Transport Auxiliary with just one hand. It's almost too hard to believe that it was possible, but it was. Well it was for that guy.

The *Belfast Telegraph* of Saturday 26 October 1940 included the following article concerning women pilots and the different type of aircraft that they were going to be allowed to fly. What the article does not include is the reason why this change was being made. Was it down to additional training, an improvement in the flying abilities of female pilots, or was it simply down to necessity? On that point, there was no clarity.

> I understand that women are to be allowed to pilot Hurricane fighters, states the *Daily Telegraph and Morning Post* air correspondent. Their task will be to take the Hurricanes from the factories to units at which equipment is added and then to fly them to the squadrons.
>
> Up to now male pilots have been solely responsible for deliveries of fighters and bombers as members of the Air Transport Auxiliary Service.
>
> The women's section of this organization have been permitted to take only training types from the factories.

The entire question of women pilots in the Air Transport Auxiliary was somewhat strange. Now before any of you cry out 'sexist', let me explain what I mean. At the time of the Second World War the structure, demands and expectations of British society, especially towards women and their purpose in life, were vastly different to what they are today. Generally, women were seen as wives, mothers and minders of the household, and any work in which they engaged was usually of a menial nature. The Second World War changed many of these stereotypes, because with so many men going off to fight in the war, the jobs that they left behind still needed to be done, and it was to women that the government and employers turned. Some simply saw the prospect of flying as a step too far for women, something that certain men of position and power saw as being beyond their basic comprehension to be able to undertake. For others it was about the encroachment into the world of masculinity by women which they either did not like, or struggled to come to terms with.

All of the initial female members of the Air Transport Auxiliary were experienced pilots who had been flying aircraft for many years, so once the decision had been made allowing female pilots to become members of the Air Transport Auxiliary, I for one do not understand why there was then any restriction placed upon them as to which aircraft they could or could not fly. It was simply absurd not to let them sit at the controls of any and all the aircraft that the men were allowed to be in charge of.

It was more to do with an outdated, male chauvinist approach to women and the position which they felt that they should fulfil in life.

The *Sunday Mirror* carried an interesting article on Sunday 17 November 1940. In the main it was written about the woman in charge of the women's section of the Air Transport Auxiliary, Pauline Gower, and those under her command.

It started off by explaining that that very same day she had flown some 400 miles with part of her journey taking her to Scotland. The following day she was due to fly another 600 miles. She certainly did lead by example and did not ask anything of her female colleagues that she wasn't prepared, willing and able to do herself, the mark of a good and well-respected leader.

A good analogy of the Air Transport Auxiliary would be that they were to the RAF what the Royal Fleet Auxiliary was to the Royal Navy.

By November 1940 the women's section of the Air Transport Auxiliary still only numbered twenty-five members in total but, despite these meagre staff numbers, in October 1940 they still managed to move hundreds of aircraft all over the country. It really was a case of just getting on with the job in hand and in the process showing that they could do the job just as competently and efficiently as their male counterparts. They just took it all in their stride.

Gower had been famous as an aviator long before the war had begun. In ten years as a taxi pilot, she had flown some 30,000 passengers to their destinations.

On Saturday 16 November 1940 Gower carried out the morning's briefing and, for her and her colleagues, it was a relatively quiet day's work. Two aircraft needed to be flown from a Midlands location to an RAF pilots' training school in the west of England. Three more aircraft needed collecting from a western factory and flying to a location in Scotland, and another was destined for the north-west of England after having been picked up from a factory in the Home Counties.

All Pauline Gower had to do was to allocate pilots to each of the jobs, get them to where they had to collect the aircraft and, after the deliveries had been made, arrange to get them picked up and brought back home before the evening was enveloped by the dark night skies. Easy, when you knew how, although the last part of that equation was extremely important, because the following day it happened all over again. If pilots weren't in the correct place, then mayhem would quickly ensue and she wouldn't have sufficient pilots in place where they should be, to get that day's jobs done.

Two of her pilots, who were waiting to take off that day, were Miss Amy Johnson and Mrs Fairweather, who were to act as her taxi pilots for the day. Several other pilots would cram themselves into each of the aircraft along with their parachutes, maps, briefcases and other essential equipment.

Nine of the women who served with the Air Transport Auxiliary at that time were married; seven had children and one of them, Mrs Fairweather, was married to another Air Transport Auxiliary pilot.

Mrs Gower said somewhat wistfully in the article.

> I don't get much time for flying nowadays. There is so much office work to be done. But if there is ever a machine to be tested, I try to do it myself, just to get ten minutes in the air. It's better than nothing.

Another of the pilots mentioned was Miss Macmillan, a woman who, before the war, had been a flying instructor at the Scottish Flying

Club. She had begun her day on Saturday 16 November 1940 flying an aircraft up to her native Scotland, quite possibly Prestwick, before being brought back to the Air Transport Auxiliary base by another of her pilot colleagues flying their air taxi. But that wasn't the end of her day, far from it, as, after a short break, she was off again; this time she had to collect an aircraft from a location in the Midlands and deliver it to a base in the west country. Her favourite place to fly was amongst the Scottish lakes and mountains, adding that, although scenic, it could also be dangerous if a pilot wasn't experienced in flying in such terrain, since the contours could change very quickly, especially when travelling at speed. But she added that so was flying in urban areas if a pilot was relatively inexperienced. 'Every Midland town looks the same from the air, and there are a bewildering number of railway lines to sort out.'

When asked by a reporter if she could distinguish the towns by smell, her reply was, 'I always think there is no smell quite like Wolverhampton. The last time I flew over it, I thought my machine was on fire.'

(A reference to the city's large industrial areas.)

Smell wasn't a good navigational aid for a pilot to rely on to find and confirm their intended destination. Miss Macmillan had in fact ordered a windproof leather mask that enclosed the whole of her face, except her eyes, to protect her from the dangers of frostbite. Flying at great speed through high winds greatly enhanced how cold it could be whilst flying at altitudes of ten and fifteen thousand feet.

Good ferry pilots didn't have adventures – at least not in the air. Instead they focused on being punctual, flying to schedule and delivering their aircraft on time before moving on to their next collection or drop off elsewhere in the country.

Miss Rosemary Rees confided to a reporter that she had been so annoyed when she flew over her cottage in the Chilterns and saw that her tenants had left the garage door open that she wrote them a letter, telling them not to do it again.

A point that Gower was rightly proud of was the women's flying record to that point, which was that they had not had one single casualty. This was even more remarkable when taking into account the fact that many of the women flew seven days a week. They were supposed to take two days off after every six days of flying, but that very rarely happened due to the women's keenness to carry on flying, weather permitting. This in turn leads to the question as to whether there was a connection between the lack of breaks these women took and the subsequent number of crashes and deaths that followed amongst women pilots.

Was the reason that they chose to fly continuously with little or no breaks down to a need or desire to prove themselves and show their doubters that flying aircraft was not only a job that they could do, but do just as good as their male counterparts?

Gower pointed out a commonly held belief at the time, which highlighted the different ways men and women were generally viewed by society.

> You know what it is? When a man pilot crashes, everybody says, 'Hard luck old man.' If a girl does the same thing they say, 'Well what can you expect of a woman?'
>
> We want people to understand that we are just an average set of girls doing a serious job of work. We're not tough, and we're not fluffy little bits either.

As the reporter continued his visit of the women's base, Mrs Fairweather's aircraft was being loaded, whilst another pilot, Miss Glass, explained, in her Irish accent, that she had begun the war as a driver with the Women's Auxiliary Air Force, but had transferred to the women's section of the Air Transport Auxiliary in January 1940 soon after it had been formed. That conversation was interrupted by the sound of the engines of Mrs Fairweather's aircraft suddenly bursting into life, and away she went.

The question was asked if having twenty-five women working together had its problems, to which Miss Gower replied:

> Not a single row. I have never had to take disciplinary action against a single pilot, and I have the authority to stop them flying and their pay for a specified period of time, if I have to, but I have never had to do so.'

Just because the morning's ferry flights had all left, it did not mean that the day's work was over. Far from it! Orders kept coming in by telephone. Pilots were leaving and arriving on shorter journeys and on smaller aircraft. It was noted by the reporter that, dressed up in their heavy flying suits, and wearing their leather flying hats and goggles, it was not possible to distinguish between men and women; they were all just pilots. An aircraft landed and a pilot climbed out, man or woman, it was impossible to tell. It was only when they removed their headgear that a glimpse of lipstick or long flowing hair made the difference between the two apparent.

The *Gloucester Journal* newspaper dated Saturday 7 December 1940 included the following article about the Air Transport Auxiliary.

The recent enormous increases in aircraft production in this country have resulted in the rapid development of Air Transport Auxiliary, one of the most interesting flying organizations in the country. It began as an improvisation, developed into a vital service, and its expansion is still continuing.

Its work, which is the 'ferrying' of all new aircraft, bombers, fighters and trainers, for the Ministry of Aircraft Production, is very complicated now that the factories under the Ministry's control are turning out such vast numbers of aircraft each week.

The aircraft when they leave the factories have still to be fitted with wireless, armament and all their incidental equipment at the RAF maintenance units before they are ready for duty. The Ferry, therefore, consists of two journeys, one from factory to maintenance unit and the second from the maintenance unit to the nominated squadron.

Some idea of the complexity of the task will be gathered if it is remembered that the many factories and maintenance units are scattered all over the United Kingdom. Delivery from any one of them may take place to any one of scores of RAF bases from Land's End to John O'Groats. The variety of aircraft, some forty different types, adds not a little to the difficulties at ATA's work.

From twenty to thirty civil pilots gathered together to assist the RAF in the first few months of the war, Air Transport Auxiliary has grown, with the help of the British Overseas Airways Corporation which is responsible for the running of it, into a huge affair of some hundreds of men and women pilots with all the attendant ground organizations of instructors, engineers and operating personnel. From ten men assisting at each of two of the RAF pilots' pools it has grown into an organization with a central control and its own pilots' pools in various parts of the country. It has thus relieved the RAF of all ferrying duties and released many men for operational duties.

Each night the central control of the Air Transport Auxiliary receives from the Ministry the ferry requirements of the next day; two bombers and one reconnaissance aircraft from A to B; four fighters C to D; three trainee aircraft E to F; and so on. These orders are considered in the light of the journeys the pilots will have to make.

The pools up and down the country receive their instructions from central control and allocate their pilots to the various collections and deliveries. Early next morning each pilot sets out to pick up his first aircraft. He travels sometimes by car, sometimes by train, but generally by one of the Air Transport Auxiliary's fleet of air taxis which have their own experienced crews. The air taxi takes six or seven pilots and, flying from factory to factory, drops them off to pick up their ferries; then it collects other pilots from aerodromes where they are waiting to go on to a new job or to return to their base.

Before reaching home at the end of a day, a pilot may have ferried a bomber, a fighter and a 'trainer' one after the other and will often have flown a thousand miles or more.

The principal qualification necessary to join Air Transport Auxiliary is 150 hours solo flying. On being accepted, pilots are given a conversion course to enable them to handle modern warplanes and are then graded for duty in relation to previous experience and adaptability.

Pilots of the Air Transport Auxiliary come from many parts of the world. Canada, America, Poland and Holland all have pilots flying alongside British comrades in this arduous and essential service. Air Transport Auxiliary, according to the pilots themselves, stands for 'Ancient and Tattered Airmen'. It is a title that bears no relation to their untiring efficiency week after week, month after month, against all hazards and in all weathers.

When reading that article I was struck not only by the number of flights and hours these brave individuals completed, it also got me to thinking that maybe, just maybe, some of their deaths were down to sheer exhaustion. Flying three or four flights a day, totalling up to maybe 1,000 miles, day after day, must have been utterly exhausting for them and, sadly for some of them, they paid the ultimate price, so determined were they to get the job done.

Saturday 18 January 1941 saw the report of Polish women who had begun flying with the Air Transport Auxiliary, with an article in the *Lancashire Evening Post*.

Polish Women Fliers

Polish women have begun flying for Britain. Two women under 30, Miss Anna Leska and Miss Wojtulanis, have started as fully qualified members of the women's section of the Air Transport Auxiliary, delivering new aircraft from factories to the RAF. The two, who were civil fliers in their own country, wrote to the Air Transport Auxiliary saying that they would like to do something for Britain.

The main story in the newspapers throughout January 1941 was to do with the Air Transport Auxiliary and the death of one of their pilots, Amy Johnson, who was believed to have drowned in the Thames Estuary.

The internationally known pilot was believed to have baled out of her aircraft which was seen to crash into the sea.

A story of personal sacrifice, about a man who wanted to do his bit the best way he could, appeared in the *Daily Mirror* on Friday 14 February 1941.

> A forty-two-year-old builder whose ambition to become an RAF pilot was thwarted by his age, but whose enthusiasm to fly for his country led him to leave a successful business to ferry planes, has now been killed on Government service.
>
> He was Mr Leslie Arthur Phillips, of Hadley Way, Winchmore Hill, London, who when war broke out tried to join the RAF as a pilot but was refused a commission.
>
> For many years he held a civilian pilot's ticket. His flying experience was extensive, and he soon heard of the Air Transport Auxiliary.
>
> A year ago he was accepted as a ferry pilot. He gave up a very successful business, left his family behind, and became a First Officer.
>
> His work was to fly new planes for the Ministry of Aircraft Production to RAF stations in all parts of Britain, and he came to love it.
>
> His brother said yesterday: 'Leslie's great desire in life was to fly, and he was thrilled with the job of ferrying planes to the RAF.'

The Ferry Pilots Appeal

Gratifying Response to Peer's Broadcast

The *Belfast Telegraph* dated Wednesday 12 March 1941 included the following article concerning enlistment in to the Air Transport Auxiliary.

There has been a most gratifying response to Monday evening's broadcast appeal by the Marquis of Londonderry, Chief Commissioner for the Civil Air Guard and ferry pilots.

Lord Londonderry appealed to those flying enthusiasts up to the age of 50 who before the war were members of the Civil Air Guard, or were in the habit of flying civil aircraft with an 'A' licence, to volunteer to ferry aircraft from factories to bases.

The Ministry has telegraphed Lord Londonderry: 'You will be glad to know that the response to your broadcast appeal on behalf of the Air Transport Auxiliary has been most gratifying. Numerous applicants have appeared personally, and the mail indicates further wide interests. Hearty congratulations and sincere thanks are hereby tendered.'

On Thursday 10 April 1941 there was a very interesting article about a member of the Air Transport Auxiliary.

Pilot-Officer Lowenstein

Millionaire buried at Twyford

Fellow members of the Air Transport Auxiliary attended the funeral last Thursday of Pilot Officer 'Bobby' Lowenstein, the millionaire owner of the Pinfold, Thorpe Satchville, who met his death as the result of an accident at an airport.

A Requiem Mass was held in the early morning at Melton Catholic church, and during the afternoon a service for Protestant friends was conducted by Father A.E. Bermingham.

The coffin lay in state in front of the altar, draped with the Belgian flag and the Union Jack. By it was a horseshoe of flowers in the Belgian colours. After the service the coffin was taken to Twyford, for the interment.

It is believed that Pilot Officer Lowenstein had only two living relatives, an aunt and an uncle, now in Biarritz who escaped from Belgium at the time of King Leopold's capitulation.

A number of mourners were in attendance including the Belgian Military Attaché and Captain Stevens of the Air Transport Auxiliary.

Saturday 3 May 1941 saw a brief article appear in the *Dundee Evening Telegraph*, and in numerous other newspapers, about the death of Captain Carill Napier.

Captain Carill Napier, of the Air Transport Auxiliary, who has died from injuries received on duty some months ago, was a son of the late Mr Montague Napier, the car and aero engine designer.

Captain Napier had been a flying enthusiast since boyhood and had made three attempts to win the King's Cup. His father died a millionaire ten years ago.

A truly amazing article appeared in the *Daily Record* dated Monday 26 May 1941. It read as follows.

Chiang Jr Aids RAF

Chang, the son of Chiang Kai Shek, the famous leader of China, is ferrying aircraft for Britain.

He volunteered on completing training at the Hamble 'Air University', which he undertook, hoping to fly in China to aid in the war against Japanese aggression.

Now he is wearing the dark blue uniform of the Air Transport Auxiliary. He is ferrying single-engine aircraft from the manufacturers to RAF stores, and will soon be promoted to flying Hurricanes and Spitfire types and then to the big stuff, including four-engined bombers.

His greatest ambition is to fly the Atlantic and join the ferry pool of the most exclusive pilots in the world, those who are flying from Canada each night at the controls of the great American bombers now rolling from the factories.

The *Gloucester Citizen* of Monday 2 June 1941 carried an article about a head-on car crash in Gloucester.

> The sequel to a collision at Brockworth was heard at Gloucestershire County Petty Sessions on Saturday when a driver was fined for careless driving.
>
> The defendant was Howard F. Powell of 40 Massey Road, Gloucester, who was summonsed for having driven a motor car in a manner dangerous to the public, and alternatively with careless driving. Mr Cyril Taynton defending, and in both cases there was a plea of not guilty.
>
> The summons for dangerous driving was dismissed, and in the other case Powell was fined £2 with 1/- special costs, and his licence endorsed.
>
> Chief Superintendent W.E. Wakefield, stating the case for the prosecution, said the proceedings arose out of an accident on the Cirencester Road at Brockworth at 12.25 am on May 10.
>
> Mr Leslie A.R. Kemp, a Second Officer in the Air Transport Auxiliary, was driving a car towards the city at 12 mph. It was alleged that, a short distance before a car driven towards him by Powell reached him, the defendant turned on his headlights and then drove to his offside, with result that a head-on collision took place. Mr Kemp tried to avoid a collision by turning into a gateway but could not do so. Visibility was restricted to 30 yards at the time. Both cars were badly damaged.
>
> In conversation it was alleged that Powell had admitted he was to blame for the accident.
>
> Evidence was given by PC Baker, PC Randell, Second Officer Kemp, Peter McCleary, an officer in the RAF, who

stated that in his opinion if Powell had exercised the same care as other drivers the accident would not have happened.

A statement was read out by PC Randell in which Powell said visibility was very bad at the time and he was under the impression he was close to the nearside kerb.

Mr Taynton, addressing the bench, stated that Powell was returning from a dance at Cheltenham. When on the Cirencester Road, visibility became so poor he decided to turn back for Cheltenham where his passenger had relations. He was proceeding very cautiously after he had turned when visibility suddenly became worse. He did not stop suddenly because of traffic which might have been behind, but began to brake. He was almost stationary when he saw the lights of a car approaching, and though he began to pull to the left he could not avoid a collision. He then realised he was on the wrong side of the road.

Mr Taynton submitted that poor visibility was the entire cause of the accident, and that his client had done all he could in the circumstances. Powell had driven for four years without previous trouble.

Announcing the decision of the Bench the chairman, Mr Stamford Hutton, observed that the magistrates took into consideration all the mitigating circumstances. They thought, however, that Powell should have carried out his duty of stopping suddenly or regaining his near side.

Saturday 19 July 1941 saw an interesting article appear in the *Newcastle Evening Chronicle*.

Dangerous mission of Jim Morrison

Mr Jim Morrison, hero of a hundred thrilling flights in the days of peace, has just completed successfully a daring flight of another nature for Air Transport Auxiliary.

He volunteered for a specially dangerous mission to fly an aircraft of unusual design and of limited range for delivery along a route which involved frequent halts for fuel, careful navigation and venturing into areas which are the preserves of the enemy.

His aircraft was unarmed but he carried a parachute.

While no details of the aircraft or of the route and destination may be given, it may be said that the Ministry of Aircraft Production were well pleased with his performance, and that the people for whom the aircraft was destined have now received it.

Jim Morrison is now flying home, this time as a passenger, on completion of his latest adventure. He will probably return to the Atlantic ferry, on which he had commenced duties, flying bombers from America to Britain when he volunteered for his special duty.

What was so special about the aircraft, why it was a dangerous mission, or where Morrison took it to was not disclosed.

Thursday 28 August 1941 saw an article appear in the *Daily Mirror* that highlighted the type of individuals that members of the Air Transport Auxiliary truly were.

This is the story of a pilot who knew no fear, until a crash robbed him of one arm and his nerve. Then he was terrified of the air, but he fought the weakness and today flies some of our fastest planes.

From the time he started flying, First Officer R.A. Corrie, of Air Transport Auxiliary, had known no fear until one day, in a plane, sickening seconds of terror crowded one on another until the crash came.

After that the man who had no fear was afraid, afraid of the thing he loved the best. For four years he fought against his dread, and when he put himself to the test, he panicked.

But he fought back. Now at 35, with his left sleeve hanging empty at his side, he has finally conquered the fear and panic.

He first became a pilot at 17 years of age, and he got his first job taking pictures from an old Avro machine. This was too slow. He started doing some crazy aerobatics. He jumped at the chance of a job in India, where his best customers were tea planters.

From there Corrie moved on to Australia and then to the United States, where he became a test pilot. A Hollywood film company heard he was to try out the last word in aeroplanes and asked whether there was a chance of thrilling pictures. 'Come on over,' invited Corrie.

Up he climbed till the watchers on the ground saw only a speck in the sky. When he put the machine into a steep dive, throttle wide open, he exulted as his plane shot like an incredible arrow towards the earth.

'And then I saw something that made me shout in horror,' he said. One of the wings cracked then sailed away from the machine. The last I remember was regretting having to die at the greatest moment of my life.

His legs, ribs, arms and skull were broken and the doctors said he could not live. But the doctors knew nothing of the valiant spirit within the poor shattered frame. Two weeks later Corrie recovered consciousness. His left arm had been amputated.

'I'll bet the movie boys got their thrilling pictures,' was how he greeted the world.

When Corrie left hospital nine months later, he agreed that his flying days were over. He came back to England, and at nights he would sometimes re-live the horror of that terrible dive. He tried to fight his fear but always he was beaten.

Four years after his crash came the war. He put his fears behind him and told his wife that he would have a shot at the

Air Transport Auxiliary. A little while later he was climbing aboard a plane with Captain Neil, who gives the men of the Air Transport Auxiliary their check flights. They soared off and Corrie took over the controls.

'I went stiff with fright,' he tells you. 'We were coming down and seeing the earth flying up to meet us, I lost my nerve. God knows how we landed.'

'As soon as the machine stopped, I wanted to run away, but Captain Neil opened the throttle and zoom, up we went again.' The quiet voice of Captain Neil breaks in, 'I've never seen anybody quite so scared in all my life,' he says.

'He told me that he would never be able to fly, but I thought otherwise. I wanted the man to beat himself and he has.'

'It was only due to his patience and perseverance that I got my wings,' says Corrie. With his one arm Corrie now ferries the fastest machines in our Air Force.

What a truly amazing story, and one that shows the calibre, inner strength and steely determination of the individuals who put themselves forward and volunteered to fly with the Air Transport Auxiliary.

Friday 5 September 1941 saw the tragic news of the death of a member of the Air Transport Auxiliary, appear in the *Scotsman*.

The death is announced, following a motor accident of Captain J.W. Stirling, who was the Chief Engineer officer to the Air Transport Auxiliary, and whose home was in Clydebank. Captain Stirling was the engineer superintendent of the European and South African sections of Imperial Airways, and when the British Overseas Airways Corporation was inaugurated he was appointed superintendent of engine production. Some months ago he was transferred to the Air Transport Auxiliary.

Saturday 22 November 1941 saw an amazing article about the Air Transport Auxiliary in the *Walsall Observer and South Staffordshire Chronicle.*

Why Plane hit Lorry

Cyclist's story of Narrow Escape when Driver was Killed

His amazing escape from being run down by an aeroplane which he had watched landing on an aerodrome was described to the Coroner at a West Midlands inquest this week, by Charles Hayden, of 20 Gladstone Street, Walsall.

After telling how he got off his bicycle and stood on the roadway to watch the aircraft land after it had circled the aerodrome several times, Haden added, 'I suddenly realised that it was coming too fast and would not be able to pull up. There was a lorry approaching and I waved and shouted to the driver to stop, but I don't think he understood me. I then saw that I was in danger myself, and as it was too late to run, I fell flat on my face on the grass verge and whilst I lay there I saw the aircraft pass over me and then heard a crash.'

The aircraft hit the lorry which Mr Hayden had tried to stop and it was completely wrecked. He found the driver lying on the ground in the hedge covered with ashes that had comprised the load. It was the driver, John Fox (22), Green Lane, Great Barr, on whom the inquest was held, and evidence showed that an Air Transport Auxiliary pilot, an American, named Jack Fitzgerald, was landing his plane on the aerodrome and when it touched down he applied the brakes, it skidded, just like a toboggan, leaving him absolutely helpless to do anything. The accident was said to have been caused by the wet grass, the aircraft having run for more than 400 yards instead of the customary 250.

Recording a verdict of accidental death, the Coroner said that the pilot was a victim of circumstances and it was more or less a case of misadventure.

The ferry pilot was among those who expressed sympathy with Fox's relatives. At his funeral at West Bromwich on Saturday following a Requiem Mass at the Church of the Holy Name, Great Barr, conducted by Father Bromley, there were numerous floral tributes, including those from the Air Transport Auxiliary and Sir Alfred McAlpine's staff.

It was quite amazing in the circumstances that the pilot of the aircraft actually survived the crash.

An article about the Air Transport Service appeared in the *Gloucester Citizen* of Saturday 24 January 1942. It made for interesting reading.

US Women for Ferry Service

New York Saturday. Miss Jaqueline Cochran announces that with the approval of the British and American Governments, she will recruit and help to train licensed pilots in the United States for the ferry service in Britain.

Those with the necessary qualifications among the 3,258 licensed women fliers in the United States will be sent to Britain as part of the Air Transport Auxiliary, and will be paid $4,000, which is about £1,000, a year, of which $25, about £6 a week would be placed in American banks.

Miss Cochran who flew a bomber from Canada to Britain last June, plans a flying tour to interview applicants in the principal cities of the United States.

The first unit of 25 fliers will receive training before leaving for Britain, and she estimates that 500 women pilots will be qualified, with an initial group starting training in three or four weeks' time.

In Britain, says Miss Cochran, the women will be under the jurisdiction of the RAF Ferry Command, and their salaries be paid by the British Government.

The *Belfast News Letter* dated Monday 21 September 1942, included a small article on page 5 about the work of the Air Transport Auxiliary.

Work of Air Transport Auxiliary

The Air Minister, Sir Archibald Sinclair, has sent a message to Air Commodore Gerard d'Erlanger, commander of the Air Transport Auxiliary, stating: 'Congratulations to Air Transport Auxiliary on the occasion of its third anniversary, and its 100,000th delivery of aircraft.'

The message means that 100,000 aircraft have been flown from one place to another inside Britain. The Air Transport Auxiliary, which has flown 300,000 miles since inception, delivers aircraft, including repaired machines from factories to RAF squadrons or storage places.

The *Gloucester Citizen* of Wednesday 9 December 1942 carried an article about the Air Transport Auxiliary.

The Minister of Aircraft Production was asked in the House of Commons today if he would consider recommending that the Air Transport Auxiliary Corps should in future be known as the Royal Air Transport Auxiliary Corps, and that the pilots should use the Royal Crown over their wings as is the case of RAF pilots.

Sir Stafford Cripps said he was fully conscious of the excellent work which the Air Transport Auxiliary was doing and he was reviewing its status. He did not consider, however, that he would be justified in adopting the course suggested.

The article did not include the information about who had asked the question, which on the surface appears a slightly unusual one, if for no other reason than that the Air Transport Auxiliary was never going to exist as an entity after the war was finally over.

On Thursday 31 December 1942 the following appeared in the *Evening Despatch*.

Cripps thanks Ferry Pilots

Sir Stafford Cripps, the Minister of Aircraft Production, has sent a New Year message to the Air Transport Auxiliary in which he expresses his most grateful thanks for the splendid work they have done in the past year.

'Their task, which is one of difficulty and danger, is an essential part of our war effort, he adds, and they have, I know, followed it through with great devotion and courage. All good luck to them.'

Saturday 23 January 1943 saw an article appear in the *Surrey Advertiser* concerning a tragic accident.

Mr Patrick Trevor-Williams

Killed in accident

The death has occurred as a result of a flying accident involving Mr Patrick Morgan Trevor-Williams, aged 22, Second Officer in the Air Transport Auxiliary, the youngest son of Mrs Clara Trevor-Williams, at present living in Puttenham. This is Mrs Trevor-William's second bereavement as a result of the war. Her son Peter was killed in Libya in June of last year.

Mr P.M. Trevor-Williams was born at East Preston, Sussex, where his father was a vicar. He was educated at

Broxham School, near Oxford. For a time after leaving school he worked for a firm of motor engineers. He joined the RAF at the outbreak of the present war and fought in the Battle of Britain as a fighter pilot. He was invalided out of the RAF in the autumn of 1941 and stayed with his mother at the home of Captain E.H. Tuckwell, in Puttenham, for a time.

Saturday 11 December 1943 saw an article appear in the *Middlesex Chronicle* concerning a serving member of the Air Transport Auxiliary.

Wearing the uniform of the Air Transport Auxiliary, 31-year-old Walter Broomhall was charged at Brentford on Thursday with being an absentee from an Army training unit since November 18th. Broomhall, who said he had not had his calling up papers, was remanded in custody to await an escort, and told he must explain the matter to his Commanding Officer.

Saturday 25 December 1943 saw an article appear in the *Cheshire Observer* about the death of a member of the Air Transport Auxiliary.

The death of Mr Alfred Denson, of 78 Beeston View, Handbridge, took place in the Royal Berkshire Hospital, Reading, on Thursday last week. Mr Denson, who was aged 17, was a son of Mr and Mrs A.B. Denson and was educated at St Mary's School, Handbridge. After leaving school Mr Denson was employed for some time with Milne and Co., seedsmen, of Chester. He was one of the original members of the 1366 Squadron of the Air Transport Auxiliary in Chester. At the time of his death he was a member of the Air Transport Auxiliary and was attending one of their courses at the time.

The funeral took place on Monday when a service at St Mary's Church, Handbridge, was conducted by Rev.

A.W. Sarson and was attended by representatives of the Air Transport Auxiliary and the Air Training Corps. Also present were Cadets Worrall and Durrant of No. 1366 squadron of the Air Training Corps.

The inquests took place of two members of the Air Transport Auxiliary. An article on the proceedings appeared in the *Surrey Advertiser* on Saturday 5 February 1944.

Plane Crash on Common

Inquest on Two Airmen

Verdicts of 'Accidental death' were recorded by the West Surrey Coroner, Mr G. Willis Taylor, at inquests at Woking on Friday last week on two airmen who lost their lives when a plane crashed on Horsell Common on Sunday 23rd January.

The pilot, Stanley Richard Herringshaw, aged 38, of Burnham, Bucks, of the Air Transport Auxiliary, was killed instantly, and the passenger, Stanley Edwin Cooke, of St John's Wood, London, died in hospital at Woking soon after admission.

Stewart Henry Paice, of Maybury Hill, Maybury, of the Army Cadet Force, said he was on Horsell Common and saw an aeroplane with its port engine smoking and later on fire. The aeroplane circled and the pilot then made a rapid descent and crashed.

When Paice and others arrived at the spot the plane was blazing fiercely. The passenger had been thrown about 30 yards from the plane.

John Crowther, Spinney View, Ottershaw, senior examiner, Aeronautical Inspection Dept., produced a certificate of airworthiness in respect of the machine.

Dr Eric Gardner said Cooke died from contusion of the brain and other multiple injuries, and the pilot from shock due to spinal injuries. The pilot, said Mr Gardner, had inhaled smoke to an unusual degree while still flying. As he was able to breath fresh air in the intervals of inhaling smoke, it would have disturbed him. That might have determined the cause of his inability to land the plane.

The *Scotsman* dated Tuesday 28 November 1944 included an article about Captain William L. Stewart having flown 100 flights across the North Atlantic.

To an Edinburgh man, Captain William L. Stewart, of British Overseas Airways Corporation, falls the distinction of being the first civilian pilot to complete 100 consecutive crossings of the North Atlantic between Montreal and Prestwick. Captain Stewart completed his century when his Liberator touched down at the big Scottish air terminal on Sunday.

Captain Stewart, who had pre-war experience with the RAF and later with Imperial Airways, flew supplies to the Advanced Air Striking Force in France and after 1940 was a member of the Air Transport Auxiliary. He was one of the pioneers who made the first arduous winter crossing of the Atlantic when the first American-built Lockheed Hudson bombers were flown to Prestwick in November four years ago.

Among the special missions with which he has been entrusted was the conveyance of General Montgomery from this country to Cairo to take up command of the Eighth Army. One hundred crossings of the North Atlantic means 330,000 miles flown, 220,000 of them over the Ocean.

Another Scot of BOAC, Radio Officer David Rennie of Stranraer, has completed a Transatlantic century. Rennie, who made his hundredth crossing from east to west, has several first flights to his credit including the first from Montreal to Moscow made via Prestwick in October 1942.

Captain Stewart's achievement was truly remarkable, one of consistent persistence and endurance. Any one of those journeys could have been his last.

Saturday 9 December 1944 saw an article appear in the *Nottingham Journal* concerning the crash of an aircraft flown by a ferry pilot of the Air Transport Auxiliary.

'A ball of fire' was the description applied to a plane which crashed at Annesley on 25 November by a female labourer employed by the LNER at Annesley, who was a witness at the inquest at Kirby yesterday on 33-year-old John Platt Murphy, of Cheadle, Cheshire, an Air Transport Auxiliary pilot, who was fatally injured when the machine crashed.

A death notice appeared in the *Surrey Mirror* of Friday 16 February 1945 concerning the death of Mr Gilbert Christopher Gould on active service.

Recently, in the service of his country, Gilbert Christopher Gould, aged 38, First Officer, Air Transport Auxiliary, precious husband and perfect lover of Esme Maude, and darling Daddy of Mary and John. Passed onwards for higher service.

Only a thin veil hangs between the pathways where we are, and God keep watch tween thee and me. This is my prayer. He holds my hand. He holdeth me, and keeps us near.

Esme.

The *Crawley and District Observer* of Saturday 24 February 1945 carried the following article about the death of First Officer Gilbert Christopher Gould.

The death occurred recently of 38-year-old First Officer Gilbert Christopher Gould of Tanglehedge, Limes Estate, Felbridge.

Always keenly interested in flying, he joined the Royal Air Force Volunteer Reserve and his period of service terminated shortly before the beginning of the war. He was one of the founder members of the Surrey Gliding Club at Redhill. It was as a Ferry Pilot in the Air Transport Auxiliary that he met his death while flying an aircraft over Southern England.

First Officer Gould was very well known in the Felbridge district. He took an active interest in local affairs. He was hon. secretary of the Parochial Church Council and at this time it was partly due to his efforts that the footpath on the church side of the road from the border up as far as Limes Estate was constructed. The laying of sewers in the district was also partly due to his agitation.

Much sympathy has been extended to his widow, who is left with a young son and daughter.

The *Newcastle Journal* dated Monday 5 March 1945 included a story about an Air Transport Auxiliary pilot, and his less than honourable behaviour.

Fliers 'at the cinema' alibi fails.

An unsuccessful alibi that he was in a Carlisle cinema at the time that he was alleged by the prosecution to be stealing poultry at Gaitsgill, eight miles away, was put forward at Carlisle on Saturday by 31-year-old Hugh Taylor of Wood Villa, Great Corby, near Carlisle, an officer of the Air Transport Auxiliary.

Taylor was ordered to pay a penalty of £55 9s on a charge of stealing poultry, valued at £27 5s, the property of Mrs Heslop, Hall Hills Farm, Gaitsgill, Dalston, and was also fined £2 for having a .22 air rifle without a firearms certificate.

Above left and above right:
Amy Johnson, CBE.
The first woman to fly
solo from London to
Australia and pilot in the
ATA during the Second
World War.

Right: Ann Welch earned
her pilot's licence when
she was just 17 years old
and enrolled in the ATA
when war broke out.
She was appointed OBE
in 1966.

ATA pilots in 1942: Jenny Broad, Audrey Sale-Barker, Gabrielle Patterson, Pauline Gower.

An example of a certificate of Commendation, presented here to Third Officer (Miss) R. Kerly.

Diana Barnato Walker, MBE. The first woman to break the sound barrier.

Diana Barnato Walker climbing in to a Spitfire.

Left: Elsie Joy Davison, the ATA female pilot to be killed in the Second World War on 8 July 1940.

Below: Pauline Gower, Margaret Cunnison, Winifred Crossley, Margaret Fairweather, Mona Friedlander, Joan Hughes, G. Patterson, Rosemary Rees.

Right: Third Officer Helen Kerly, photographed as a member of the Royal Aero Club in 1938. One of only two women to be commended as a pilot during the war.

Below: Avro 504J aircraft. Flown by members of the ATA.

Avro Anson. A bomber-type aircraft flown by members of the ATA during the course of the Second World War.

Burnelli UB-14. One of the more unusual aircraft flown by members of the ATA.

Captain Joan Hughes, MBE. She was the youngest female pilot to join the ATA, doing so when she was 21 years of age in 1940.

Faith Bennett signing to collect a spitfire. Throughout the 1930s she appeared in a number of British films but joined the ATA in 1941.

Above: Five ATA flyers; Lettice Curtis, Jenny Broad, Audrey Sale-Barker, Gabrielle Patterson and Pauline Gower.

Left: James A. Mollison, MBE. A Pioneering Scottish aviator who was married to Amy Johnson.

Above left: John Gulson, a flight engineer with the ATA, was awarded the George Medal in July 1944 for saving the crew of a Halifax bomber which crashed at White Waltham.

Above right: Avro Anson Camera Install, July1944.

Below: Pauline Gower in a de Havilland Tiger Moth at Hatfield, Hertfordshire, 10 January 1940.

Above: Wellington Bombers.

Left: Robert Smith-Barry (right). During the First World War he served as a major in the RFC and the RAF.

Right: Third Officer
Margaret Frost who
joined the ATA on
25 November 1942.

Below: The initial
course of the ATA,
looking over a map.

Above left: A booklet given to all pilots who served with the ATA.

Above right: Marion Wilberforce, one of the original group of ATA pilots.

Below: The original members of the Unit: Pauline Gower, Winifred Crossley, Margaret Cunnison, Margaret Fairweather, Mona Friedlander, Joan Hughes, Gabrielle Patterson, Rosemary Rees, Marion Wilberforce.

Four pilots of the ATA during the Second World War.

Pilot flying badge of the ATA.

ATA pilots beginning their days work.

Three members of the ATA checking parachutes before take off.

Members of No. 2 Ferry Pool ATA Whitchurch, Bristol.

Two ATA pilots having just delivered a de Havilland Mosquito.

A pilot preparing for a flight.

For the prosecution it was alleged that a boy employed by Mrs Heslop saw Taylor, who had a black moustache, carrying poultry near Hall Hills after gun shots had been heard. Other witnesses said they saw a car, which answered the description of Taylor's in the Gaitsgill district and that the driver was like Taylor. A police officer who examined the car found feathers in it.

Taylor, who admitted to a Police Inspector that he had shaved off his moustache, told magistrates that he had started to trim it, but as that was not a success he decided to shave it off altogether.

He said that his car must have been taken away by someone else from a Carlisle garage while he was in the cinema.

An expert witness from the Home Office forensic laboratory at Preston, said that a spent shot found at the place where the poultry were missing from, had been shot from a gun found in Taylor's car.

The *Liverpool Evening Express* of Saturday 21 April 1945 reported that an aircraft had crashed in a field at Taplow near Maidenhead on the evening of Friday 20 April. A woman pilot and an Air Training Corps cadet were both killed, the aircraft having burst into flames when it crashed into the ground. The victims were 28-year-old Third Officer Leslie Cairns Murray, a single woman, and Air Training Corps Cadet Geoffrey Bernard Regan from Staines, in Middlesex.

What made the tragedy even more poignant was that the dead cadet's father, George Arthur Regan, was a chief engineer at the unnamed aerodrome from where the aircraft had taken off. Leslie Cairns Murray lived with her parents, Ian and Mary Murray, at Charing Cross in London. She was buried in Chislehurst cemetery in Kent. The inscription on her headstone is, 'I bear you on eagle wings and brought you unto myself.'

Wednesday 30 May 1945 saw an article appear in the *Gloucestershire Echo* concerning a crash involving Reginald John Richard Jackson.

First Officer R.J.R. Jackson

Missing After Air Crash

Mrs R.J.R. Jackson, of 54 Eldon Road, Cheltenham, Gloucestershire, has received news that her husband, First Officer Reginald John Richard Jackson, Air Transport Auxiliary, is missing following an air crash while on a ferry flight.

First Officer Jackson, who is 36 years of age, was a member of the Cotswold Aero Club before the war and joined the Royal Air Force in 1941.

In 1942 he transferred to the Air Transport Auxiliary. His parents live at 45 St George's Street, Cheltenham, Gloucestershire. He had a young son.

Friday 13 July 1945 didn't bring any bad luck for Second Officer and Flight Engineer John Gulson – in fact quite the opposite, as he was awarded the George Medal. The announcement was made in the *Nottingham Journal* on the same day.

In June 1944 a Halifax bomber crashed into the railway cutting at the Air Transport Auxiliary's White Waltham headquarters. Unbeknown to staff at White Waltham, the Halifax was fully loaded with bombs. The potential loss of life and damage to surrounding property would have been devastating.

For his part in the rescue of the crew of the stricken Halifax, John Gulson was awarded the George Medal whilst putting his own life at risk in doing so.

One of the Air Transport Auxiliary's most experienced short distance ferry pilots was 27-year-old Miss Diana Ramsey. On Thursday 16 August 1945 an article appeared about her in the *Good Morning* newspaper.

For five years during the course of the Second World War her job was to fly very powerful aircraft all over the country, which understandably had left her with quite a few stories to tell about her experiences.

One such story involved her landing at an airfield in a Tempest fighter aircraft only to discover that the throttle on her aircraft had jammed whilst she was flying at 130 miles per hour. There was nothing else she could do other than cut the engine of her aircraft, keep her fingers crossed and hope for the best. The plane shot across the airfield, and carried on for some two miles before crashing into some trees with such force that it knocked one of them down, but that didn't stop the aircraft; it carried on across a ploughed field, losing its tail in the process, before it finally came to a rest after crashing into a copse.

Conscious and uninjured, other than a few scratches and bruises, Diana Ramsey turned round to see that nearly all of her aircraft had been left embedded in the trees she just ploughed through. Basically all that was left of her aircraft was the cockpit she was sitting in. An ambulance and a fire engine were quickly on the scene to Ramsey's assistance. But before she allowed herself to be taken away in the ambulance for medical attention, she showed her human and caring side, by chasing away some inquisitive cows who had gathered around the wreckage of her aircraft, to ensure that none of them came to any harm.

The *Nottingham Journal* carried an article on Monday 3 September 1945 about the wedding of two members of the Air Transport Auxiliary.

The Bishop of Egypt, the Right Rev. L.H. Gwynne, assisted by Canon W.E. Ives, officiated at the wedding of two Air Transport Auxiliary officers at St Andrew's Church, Nottingham, on Saturday. They were Third Officer Bernard Knight Wadsworth, flight engineer, only son of Mr and Mrs Edward Wadsworth, of Rushden, Northants, and Third Officer

Eleanor Dorothy Fish, ferry pilot, elder daughter of Mrs and the late Mr George F. Fish of Pelham Road, Nottingham.

Before joining the Air Transport Auxiliary in January 1942, the bride was an architect with a local firm. Flight Captain A.J. Spiller, also of the Air Transport Auxiliary, was the best man and the reception was held at the George Hotel.

After the war ended, everybody had to get back to normality the best way that they could. It was a time of change for many people. For those who worked for the Air Transport Auxiliary it was no different. Friday 12 October 1945 saw an article appear in the *Bucks Herald* on just that very topic.

A new personality, a lady rider, will soon be joining the country's hunting, jumping and gymkhana fraternity. She is Mrs Peggy Eveleigh, who was Master of the North Somerset Foxhounds during the 1940 season. She has done a lot of riding both in the USA and this country before the war. Now she has left her wartime job of ferry-pilot with the Air Transport Auxiliary at Haddenham airfield and is setting up hunting stables and a riding school at Bierton, Aylesbury. While in America she contributed to the *Milwaukee Journal* as an expert on horsemanship. She intends making flying her peacetime hobby.

It is quite amazing how many wartime Air Transport Auxiliary pilots continued flying in some capacity after the war.

The war, as if proof was needed, showed just how unfair life could be. Sadly, that was the case for one member of the Air Transport Auxiliary. An account of the incident appeared in the *Gloucester Citizen* on Tuesday 30 October 1945.

A mishap during the merry-making at the closing down of the Air Transport Auxiliary at Ratcliffe aerodrome, near

Leicester, cost the life of Flying Officer Henry Ernest Spain, who had come especially from Prestwick, Ayrshire, for the occasion.

Three officers were standing toasting each other when a glass chanced to catch Spain on the eye. It broke and the eye was badly cut.

Spain was taken to Leicester Infirmary, some miles away, and doctors got busy at once, but he collapsed and died. He was 22 years of age and lived at Sandwich, Kent.

With the end of the war came the end of the role of the ferry pilots of the Air Transport Auxiliary. On Monday 3 December 1945 their wartime role was handed back to the pilots of the RAF. An article to this effect appeared in the *Yorkshire Post and Leeds Intelligencer* the very same day.

Ferry Pilots Job Ends as RAF Take Over From

Air Transport Auxiliary

A notable war service comes to an end today when the Air Transport Auxiliary hand back to the Royal Air Force the task of ferrying military aircraft. Since July the RAF have been collecting their own aircraft from storage and maintenance units, and today they take over collection from the factories and the Air Transport Auxiliary ceases to exist.

When the Commanding Officer, Commodore Gerard d'Erlanger, formed the organization in September 1939 it was expected that the Air Transport Auxiliary's chief function would be that of an emergency communications flight. The 26 enthusiastic amateur pilots, all too old or unfit for service with the RAF, who joined Commodore d'Erlanger at the start did not expect to handle other than light types of aircraft with which they were familiar. Like most amateur flying men of that time few had handled a fast single- or twin-engine military type.

But their love of flying and their determination to tackle any task outweighed their lack of experience, and when they were invited to assist the RAF in ferrying military aircraft from factory to maintenance units and operational stations, they responded readily.

During the Battle of Britain, when the RAF were too occupied to do any more ferrying themselves, the Air Transport Auxiliary were ready to take on the entire job.

Since that time Air Transport Auxiliary pilots have ferried every type of British and American military aircraft. They have made over 300,000 deliveries and handled over 200 different types.

From their early days as a small part of the RAF Ferry Pools at Hucknall and Filton, the Air Transport Auxiliary expanded to an organization of over 700 pilots and flight engineers and 3,000 ground staff with their own airfield and headquarters at White Waltham, in Berkshire, and with 14 of their own ferry pools throughout England, Scotland and Northern Ireland.

The distinctive navy-blue RAF-style uniform of the Air Transport Auxiliary became well known in all parts of the British Isles.

Men and women from France, Poland, Malaya, Switzerland, Estonia, China and almost every other Allied country served in the Air Transport Auxiliary. To train such a cosmopolitan group an entirely new technique had to be applied. Aircraft were divided into six categories, ranging from simple single-engine types (Class I) to the heaviest four-engined bombers (Class V) and flying boats (Class VI), and pilots were allotted to those classes according to their experience and competence. A series of technical publications and bulletins was produced, written in simple language and aimed at giving the ferry pilots the bare details that they required to fulfil their task.

Only in the direst circumstances have Air Transport Auxiliary pilots 'baled out' and sacrificed their machines. Perhaps many of the 150 pilots and flight engineers who lost their lives during the six years might have survived had they not tried to save their aircraft. The accident rate has been remarkably low. Only one-third of one per cent of Air Transport Auxiliaries deliveries have resulted in any kind of mishap, however trivial.

Air Transport Auxiliaries ferried to France before the fall of that country in the summer of 1940, and they were there again soon after the first airstrips were laid in Normandy last year. Since then they have provided an important communications link with the Continent, flown urgent medical and other supplies to Holland, Belgium, France, Germany, Austria, Czechoslovakia and Italy, and their air ambulances have brought relief to wounded of all countries.

And now, their job completed, the Air Transport Auxiliary are being disbanded. But their tradition will be carried on by the members in airlines and flying clubs throughout the new world. After six years of the sweat and toil of ferry work, Air Transport Auxiliary pilots are still eager to fly.

The *Motherwell Times* of Friday 11 January 1946 carried news of the New Year's Honours' List which included the name of one man who had served with the Air Transport Auxiliary during the Second World War.

The article reported on Mr James McGuiness, who had been the Officer Commanding No. 4 Ferry Pool section of the Air Transport Auxiliary, stationed at Prestwick, Scotland. For his wartime service he was appointed OBE. Mr McGuiness was a native of Motherwell.

Mr McGuiness was also a veteran of the First World War, having served with No. 39 Squadron of the Royal Flying Corps, whose job it was to protect London from German Gotha bombers and the large Zeppelin airships which had been tasked with carrying out air raids over London and the south-east of England.

He had served with the Air Transport Auxiliary since May 1940. At 48 years of age, he was married with four children – a daughter, and three sons – one of whom was still serving with the RAF in 1946.

An interesting story appeared in *The Scotsman* on Tuesday 12 November 1946 concerning an ex-member of the Air Transport Auxiliary who, having returned from his wartime service, settled at The Meadows, Kilmalcolm, where he carried on work as a yarn merchant.

> A fine of £240 was imposed on John Richard Wainwright MacLaurin, yarn merchant, The Meadows, Kilmacolm, when he admitted carrying out repair and decoration work to his house and two garages without having obtained a licence from the Ministry of Works, at Greenock yesterday. Sheriff Bonnar stated that the fine, which was the equivalent amount spent on the work, was the minimum he could impose. It was explained by an agent that Mr MacLaurin had been on service with the Air Transport Auxiliary for more than three years. When he returned, the house was badly needing repairs and, unaware of the regulations, he had the work carried out.

Mr MacLaurin's treatment by the authorities appears to be somewhat harsh. I appreciate that these rules were there to be applied fairly and squarely to everybody, but you would have thought that there was room for the use of common sense in the circumstances.

The *Harrogate Herald* carried an interesting article about ex-Air Transport Auxiliary pilot Mr H.L. Brook in their edition of Wednesday 1 October 1947.

> In Harrogate this weekend was H.L. Brook, the famous Harrogate airman who broke the England to Australia for light aircraft in 1937 and twice attacked the record for the flight to the Cape.

Flying is a thing of the past for him now. 'I've been farming in Devon since 1941,' says this Harrogate man, 'and I think I'll take another farm and go back to the land.'

But inside this quiet modest man there still stirs the spirit which made him, in the days when aircraft were still being developed, a 'nine days' wonder', as he calls it.

'Often when I hear of the record to the Cape being broken by the RAF, I have a sneaking feeling that I might get a plane and have a crack at it just for fun,' he says.

With no flying time since he left the Air Transport Auxiliary in 1941, Mr Brook feels somewhat out of touch with modern flying. 'All these pilotless planes, flying bombs etc., make one wonder if even flying itself will not become obsolete,' he laments.

Next attraction for him after farming is emigration. 'It's difficult to know what to do in this country just now,' he says, 'but it's a very great temptation many times to get into our motor cruiser and sail her to South Africa.'

Mr Brook's exploits in the air have now been forgotten by most of the public, but he still gets a sort of reflected glory from a namesake, H.L. Brook, the motor-car racer. 'I often get his mail, and he gets mine,' he says, 'and people often ask me how I like motor racing after aircraft racing.'

A clear message that the war was well and truly over, as if one was needed by the latter months of 1947, was an advertisement which appeared in the *Falkirk Herald* on Saturday 22 November 1947 for wartime surplus uniform and kit that was no longer needed for its original and intended purposes.

One could purchase 'Ladies Motoring Gloves' which apparently made an 'ideal Christmas present'. The description of them was as follows.

Brand new, large gauntlet, very best quality yellow leather, fleecy lined palms and fingers, gauntlet leather lined.

Guaranteed perfect quality. Suitable for business, dress wear
or motoring, sizes 6 and a half or 7. Price 39/6d, postage 6d.

Having seen the advert's accompanying drawing, it is hard to visualise a
woman wearing a pair of these 'gauntlets' on a Saturday night out in her
party dress. However, if she were to become involved in 'jousting' then
they would be an extremely useful addition to her outfit.

Some of the other items included naval jackboots, ladies' blouses,
army blankets, army boots, winter overcoats, haversacks, despatch riders'
three-quarter-length jackets and Air Transport Auxiliary jackets in:

> very best quality navy blue, all wool, tricoline material,
> lovely fine quality, smart collar and lapel style with four
> patch pockets, back vent, all round belt stitched at back, art,
> silk lined. Very suitable for GTC or Girl Guide uniforms,
> etc. 32, 34, 36, 38 bust, 35/-. Slightly worn but clean and in
> first rate condition; post 10d.

On Monday 23 February 1948, the *Lincolnshire Echo* carried the
following concerning Mr Frank W. Bell, a wartime pilot with the Air
Transport Auxiliary.

Lincoln Firm's new Director

> Mr Frank W. Bell, export manager of Robey and Co. Ltd.,
> Lincoln, has been appointed a director of the company. He
> is the younger son of Mr W.T. Bell, chairman and managing
> director of the firm.
>
> Since commencing his apprenticeship with the company
> in 1923, he has occupied positions both in a technical and
> sales capacity, and for some years prior to the war was the
> company's export manager, during which time he carried
> out an extensive tour abroad for the company.

During the war he volunteered for the Air Transport Auxiliary, serving with them on flying duty with all types of aircraft.

This was just another example of the post-war influence, that both men and women who had undertaken wartime service with the Air Transport Auxiliary possessed.

On the back page of the *Daily Mirror* of Tuesday 13 April 1948 was a small article about a wartime member of the Air Transport Auxiliary.

Airway Chief fined for Flying Offence

For flying a plane in the dark without proper lights, the founder of the Air Transport Auxiliary, Captain George Stanley Pine, of Leach Farm, St Anne's, Lancashire, was fined £5 and ordered to pay £14 13s costs at Lytham, Lancashire, yesterday.

Captain Pine was described as managing director of Pine's Airways Ltd, of Squires Gate, Blackpool.

Pine had formed his company in 1936 when it was originally situated just outside Porthcawl in Wales and consisted of two Fox Moth aircraft. After his wartime service with the Air Transport Auxiliary he restarted his pleasure flight company, but this time at Squires Gate, Blackpool, with two Auster aircraft. He was later appointed MBE for his wartime service.

Tuesday 6 July 1948 saw an article included in the newspaper under the heading:

Scotland Loses Air Pioneer

Captain E.E. Fresson, who was dismissed by British European Airways from the office of Manager of Highland air routes, is to take up an executive position in Kenya.

'I shall leave Scotland with a heavy heart,' said the Captain yesterday. 'I have made so many loyal and trusted friends. I am overwhelmed by the esteem and warmth of feeling which the Scottish people, public bodies and press have expressed since the announcement in March that I was to be deprived of my livelihood without just cause.

That goodwill which the people of Scotland have shown me will always be my treasured possession. The harsh act of those whom the Government put in charge of Britain's airways always made it impossible for me to continue with aviation in this country. Private enterprise has come to the rescue and offered me a position in a country where individual effort is still of value.'

Captain Fresson believed the British Civil aviation set-up was far too rigid and was designed on extravagant service Air Transport Auxiliary methods which discouraged individual enterprise with disastrous financial results. Until those in charge changed their outlook, losses would continue to increase.

Captain Fresson was clearly not a happy individual about the way he was treated and, it would appear, with justification. A story in the *Western Morning News* of Monday 30 August 1948 caught my eye:

Devon Woman Reaches 313 mph in Spitfire

A Devon woman, Miss Lettice Curtis, in the Lympne (Kent) high-speed handicap on Saturday, set up a new international women's record for the 100 kilometres closed circuit, doing 313.07 mph in a Spitfire XI, owned by the United States Embassy.

The handicap race took place over four laps of a twenty-mile course from Lympne to Folkestone, along the sea front to Hythe and back to Lympne airport. Unfortunately for Miss Curtis, even though she set a new speed record for a woman, she did not win the race. That honour went to Flight Lieutenant Colquhoun who managed a speed of 324 mph, which won him the Hythe Aero Trophy and a cheque for £100.

> During the war Miss Curtis, who is 33 and one of six 'flying sisters' became known as one of the finest women pilots by her work with the Air Transport Auxiliary. Now, with more than 3,000 flying hours to her credit, she works as a pilot for the Ministry of Supply's aircraft and armament experimental establishment. Miss Curtis beat the previous record, set up in 1940, by 21 miles an hour.

It was nice to see that three years after the end of the Second World War, not only was the Air Transport Auxiliary still getting a mention, but pilots who had flown as its members were still flying and, in Miss Curtis's case, making a living out of it.

Mr Gerard d'Erlanger, who had commanded the Air Transport Auxiliary, was involved in circumstances beyond his control in February 1949 when it became a case of resign or be sacked from his position as chairman of British European Airways. The incident had become a political hot potato with politicians demanding to know what had actually happened.

It was announced by the Minister of Civil Aviation that Mr d'Erlanger had retired, but this wasn't believed totally by all politicians, many of whom considered that he had been sacked and were demanding to know why. He had been replaced by 55-year-old retired Marshal of the Royal Air Force Lord Douglas who, at the time, was a Labour peer. The suspicion was that d'Erlanger had been sacked because he didn't see eye to eye with Lord Pakenham at the Ministry of Civil Aviation over the direction that civil aviation should take.

On Friday 25 March 1949 there was a memorial service at St Cuthbert's Church, Bedford, for Captain P.C. Golding who had been killed in a plane crash on the 15th, as he attempted to land his aircraft at Gatow Airport, Berlin, during the post-war aerial operation known as the 'Berlin Airlift', which took place between 24 June 1948 and 12 May 1949.

This was the first major international crisis of what was known as the Cold War. During the post-war occupation of Germany by Allied nations, the Soviet Union blocked all Western Allies from entering Berlin by road, rail or canal. A joint operation to get much-needed supplies through to the residents of Berlin was begun by the RAF, followed by the Americans, and which saw pilots from America, France, Britain, Canada, New Zealand, Australia and South Africa, fly more than 200,000 flights into the beleaguered city with daily supplies which, at its peak, reached nearly thirteen tons of essential supplies.

Captain Golding, of 53 Phillpotts Avenue, Bedford, had flown with No. 6 Ferry Pool of the Air Transport Auxiliary during the course of the Second World War. Wartime colleagues who attended the memorial service included Mr F.G. Gill, Mr C.S. Clarke and Mr W.F. Castle.

Golding, one of three members of the crew of an Avro York transport who were killed when it crashed, was a married man with two children. He had worked for the owners of the aircraft, Skyways Airlines Ltd, for two and a half years.

The crash was the first involving a civil aircraft involved in the Berlin Airlift. Prior to this, ten Britons and twenty-eight Americans had been killed in accidents involving military aircraft during the 265 days of the airlift.

An article in the *Belfast News Letter* on Saturday 23 April 1949 showed just how far reaching was the influence of the Air Transport Auxiliary, with its legacy continuing long after the war was over.

The sad thing about this article is that the name of the pilot concerned is unknown.

Bid to Save Woman's Life

Drug flown from New York to England

A Pan American Airways Clipper from New York touched down at London Airport last night with a supply of a rare drug to try to save the life of a woman who, on Thursday, was given only 48 hours to live without it.

The drug, Intraheptol, contained in a small cardboard box, was transferred to a waiting plane piloted by a woman, a former Air Transport Auxiliary pilot, and rushed to Hereford airfield. There a car took it to Herefordshire County Hospital, a mile away, where the sick woman lay.

When doctors said her life could be saved only by the drug, an urgent call was made to Pan-American Airways' London office, and Intraheptol, a liver-extract drug, was packed in an icebox and placed on the Clipper leaving New York on Thursday night.

The *Dundee Evening Telegraph* of Wednesday 27 April 1949 included the following sad news about the death of an ex-Air Transport Auxiliary member.

The death in Durban, South Africa, of the man who devised the RAF's system of flying training, Mr Robert Smith Barry, is announced today. He was 63 years of age.

As a Colonel in the Royal Flying Corps in 1916 during the course of the First World War, he revolutionised the methods of training pilots and his 'Gosport system' remains basically unaltered. It has been copied by every major air power.

In September 1939 he passed his flying medical test and enlisted as an acting pilot officer in the RAF. For the Air Transport Auxiliary he ferried 400 mile per hour fighters. Injured in a crash in 1942, he was advised to live in a warm climate.

It was in December 1916 that he finalised his new flying instruction methods. The curriculum for the lessons involved combined classroom instruction along with actual hands on aircraft flight instruction. Students were exposed to potentially dangerous aerial manoeuvres, but in a controlled environment, so that they could learn quickly and remember what not to do if they wanted to stay alive, and to develop their built-in survival skills so that they could readily, and immediately recover from their errors. The aircraft of choice for putting the trainees through their paces was the Avro 504J.

Barry had qualified as a pilot in 1911 at Salisbury Plain, and he was one of the first pilots to enlist in the newly-formed Royal Flying Corps in August 1912.

With the outbreak of the First World War, Barry was appointed as a flying officer on 5 August 1914, but only 9 days later, whilst on active service in France with No. 5 Squadron, Royal Flying Corps, on 14 August, Barry's aircraft, a Royal Air Factory BE.8, had engine failure and it crashed behind enemy lines, killing his passenger in an accident that saw him sustain two broken legs, but he still somehow managed to make good his escape before he was captured by the Germans.

The following year, on 5 November 1915, he was promoted to the rank of Temporary Captain, which was made a permanent promotion less than a month later. On 3 July 1916 he was made a temporary Major; this was followed by a further promotion to that of Wing Commander and temporary Lieutenant-Colonel, on 23 August 1917. Near the war's end in 1918, he was awarded the Air Force Cross,[1] which was presented for 'an act or acts or exemplary gallantry while flying, though not in active operations against the enemy'.

Somewhat ironically he died as a result of an operation on one of his legs that had troubled him since his crash behind enemy lines in 1914.

---

[1] It was introduced on 3 June 1918.

Saturday 30 July 1949 saw an article appear in the *Gloucestershire Echo* about Miss Roy Mary Sharpe, an ex-Air Transport Auxiliary pilot, yet another example of a wartime pilot who had continued flying in the years after the war.

> She enrolled in the Civil Air Guard, and was the first member of the Cotswold Aero Club to get her licence under the scheme in November 1938. In this she defeated 50 men and 8 women.
>
> On the outbreak of war she joined the WAAF as a driver, having had only ten hours solo flying and being ineligible for the Air Transport Auxiliary. She was eventually commissioned into the WAAF. Then, in 1941, she was accepted in the Air Transport Auxiliary and flew all types of aircraft in that service until 1945, amassing a staggering 2,500 flying hours in the process.
>
> During her service with the Air Transport Auxiliary, for which she was awarded the MBE in 1946, Miss Sharpe ferried about 1,030 aircraft before being posted to the Air Movements Flight at White Waltham, near Maidenhead, when she was employed on flying Anson aircraft with passengers and freight to Europe.
>
> On leaving the Air Transport Auxiliary at the end of the war she joined the staff of Control Commission in Germany and spent some time flying Red Cross and other stores to Europe and bringing back individuals who had become displaced persons. After this she acquired a job with W.S. Shackleton Aeronautical Consultants for whom she tested and demonstrated aircraft to prospective buyers, flying them near London.

On Saturday 6 August 1949 a wedding took place at St Giles' Cathedral, Edinburgh, which not only saw large crowds in attendance, but more than 1,000 guests. The bridegroom was the Earl of Selkirk, Nigel

71

Douglas-Hamilton, brother of the Duke of Hamilton, and the bride was Miss Audrey Drummond-Sale-Baker.

The Earl had served in the RAF throughout the Second World War, whilst his wife had served with the Air Transport Auxiliary and continued her flying after the war with the Women's Royal Air Force.

The *Yorkshire Post and Leeds Intelligencer*, dated Monday 15 August 1949, included a brief article about an ex-Air Transport Auxiliary pilot, Mr Arthur J. Record.

> Other members of the Yorkshire Gliding Club who made the most of Saturday's good soaring conditions, included Mr Arthur J. Record, of Oakwood, Leeds, a former Fleet Air Arm and Air Transport Auxiliary pilot.
>
> Mr Record, who flew solo in a glider for the first time only two weeks ago, was above cloud, and reached a height of 4,000 feet in a flight of one and a half hours.

On Saturday 23 September 1950 a memorial was unveiled in St Paul's Cathedral to the men and women of the Air Transport Auxiliary who gave their lives during the course of the Second World War. The memorial is in the cathedral's Nelson crypt and commemorates the men and women from all nations who volunteered to fly the Royal Air Force's aircraft from the factories to the squadrons, and in many cases squadrons situated abroad.

On the Roll of Honour appears the name of Geoffrey Bernard Regan from Staines, who was just 16 years of age when he was killed whilst flying with a female pilot in an RAF aircraft at Maidenhead, Kent in April 1945. During the latter stages of the war a number of Air Training Corps cadets were recruited into the Air Transport Auxiliary organization to act as pilots' assistants to operate emergency controls on the latest type of RAF aircraft. These cadets flew in their ATC uniforms, and it was on one such flight that Cadet Regan was killed on active service, a fact that has been recognised by his interment at the London Road, Staines, cemetery in a war service grave.

Chapter Three

Air Transport Auxiliary – Questions in Parliament

The subject of the Air Transport Auxiliary, and the men and women who served in it, came up for discussion on numerous occasions in the House of Commons during the course of the war. Here are those discussions as recorded in Hansard.

On 6 March 1940 there was a question asked of the Secretary of State for Air about the terms of conditions for both men and women who wanted to enlist in the Air Transport Auxiliary.

Miss Irene Ward, then Conservative Member of Parliament for Wallsend in North Tyneside (she would later go on to become the MP for Tynemouth, and a life peer, as Baroness Ward of North Tyneside) asked the Secretary of State for Air whether, in view of the publicity given to the appointment of the Air Transport Auxiliary, he would define the terms of service for both men and women who had or who wanted to join.

The Minister of State for Air, Sir (Howard) Kingsley Wood, gave the following response: 'As the answer is somewhat detailed, I will, with my honourable friend's permission, circulate it in the official report.'

The relevant information was as follows:

The Air Transport Auxiliary is administered by British Airways.

(1). The Age limits.

Men.

Twenty-eight to fifty years of age, but applicants must be ineligible for operational service with the Royal Air Force.

Women.

Twenty-two to forty-five years of age.

(2). Basis of employment.

Men.

Under contract with British Airways Limited on a three-monthly basis.

Women.

Under contract with British Airways Limited on a monthly basis.

(3). Tests.

Men.

A preliminary flying test and a conversion course at the Central Flying School to determine suitability to fly military style aircraft.

Women.

A practical flying test by British Airways Limited to determine suitability to fly light training types of aircraft.

(4). Grading and remuneration.

Men.

Category A – Suitable to fly all types. Grading, First Officer. Basic salary, £350 per annum. Consolidated flying pay, £15 per month.

Category B – Suitable to fly single engine service type aircraft. Grading, First Officer. Basic salary £350 per annum. Consolidated flying pay, £10 per month.

Category C – Suitable to fly training types of aircraft only. Grading, Second Officer. Basic salary £285 per annum. Consolidated flying pay, £10 per month.

Women.

Grading, Second Officer. Basic salary £230 per annum.
Consolidated flying pay £8 per month.

Sir Kingsley did not see out the war, dying suddenly at his London home on 21 September 1943 at 62 years of age.

On 2 July 1941, Mr George Garro Jones, later to be Lord Trefgarne, asked the Secretary of State for Air by what amount the pay of a pilot who flew aircraft on active service fell short of the pay of the Air Transport Auxiliary service ferry pilot who delivered military aircraft from factories to Royal Air Force aerodromes?

In reply, Sir Archibald Sinclair who had served as a major in the Guards Machine Gun Regiment on the Western Front during the First World War and as Winston Churchill's second in command when Churchill commanded 6th Royal Scots Fusiliers in the Ploegsteert Wood sector in Flanders in 1916, replied that as the answer was long, and contained detailed figures, he would, with his honourable friend's agreement, circulate it in the official report.

Mr George Garro Jones decided to push the point by suggesting to Sir Archibald that the pilots who flew aircraft from the factories to the stations received almost twice as much as pilots of the Royal Air Force who flew military aircraft on operational duties.

Sir Archibald's response was to ask Mr Jones that, rather than ask him to make a calculation by mental arithmetic, he would be prepared to wait until he saw his report.

Mr George Garro Jones appeared to have a 'bee in his bonnet' about the Air Transport Auxiliary as he asked more than one question that day about the organization. His question on this occasion was whether the Minister of Aircraft Production contemplated any changes in the relationship of the Air Ministry and the Air Transport Service?

Lieutenant Colonel John Moore-Brabazon, who had served in the First World War, in both the Royal Flying Corps and the Royal Air Force and had been awarded the Military Cross on 1 January 1917, responded by saying that he presumed that his honourable friend was referring to the Air Transport Auxiliary Service and, if that were the case, then the answer was 'no'.

Mr George Garro Jones kept pushing the point. This time he wanted to know why was it necessary for this service to be performed by civilian workers? And was the Air Auxiliary Transport Service (the second time he had got the name wrong) really our old friend British Overseas Airways, and would it not be better to just admit that was the case.

Moore-Brabazon explained that it was in fact a totally different organization and comprised pilots who were operationally unfit, and said that it was a great relief to the Royal Air Force that we can deploy pilots on this work who cannot be employed as pilots in the Royal Air Force.

Mr George Garro Jones continued, but by now sounding more like a second-rate solicitor than a Member of Parliament. He suggested to Moore-Brabazon that the people who were responsible for employing the pilots of the Air Transport Auxiliary did so at a very large profit over what they paid to the Air Ministry.

Mr Garro Jones had quite clearly not researched the facts of his question before he had asked it, leaving Moore-Brabazon an easy task in answering the question, by explaining that the Air Transport Auxiliary came under the Ministry of Air Production, of which he was in charge. This made him ultimately responsible for the delivery of military aircraft to the Royal Air Force.

Mr George Garro Jones finished the discussion by informing Lieutenant Colonel Moore-Brabazon that, as he had been unable to receive a sufficiently detailed response to his question from the various ministers concerned, he was giving notice that he would raise the same matter on the adjournment.

Mr George Garro Jones began a discussion in the House of Commons on 29 July 1941 when he asked a question of the Minister of Aircraft Production, on what basis or calculation was the Air Transport Auxiliary paid for each aircraft it delivered to or on behalf of the Royal Air Force?

Mr Montague, the Parliamentary Secretary to the Minister of Aircraft Production, replied that the Air Transport Auxiliary had no revenue.

The cost of the organization fell on the Vote of the Ministry of Aircraft Production and that no payment was made on the basis of the number of aircraft delivered.

Jones responded by further asking whether the cost of the organization included any interest paid for the shares of British Airways on their fixed interest-bearing securities.

Mr Montague informed Mr Jones that the cost of the Air Transport Auxiliary was borne on the Vote, and asked that, if he had any questions to put concerning higher policy, perhaps he would be good enough to raise them on the appropriate Vote.

Looking back on these questions, quite a few of which appear to have been posed by Mr Garro Jones, Member for Aberdeen North, they seem somewhat strange. There was a war on, Britain had been on the brink of utter defeat early in that war, and the work that was carried out by the men and women of the Air Transport Auxiliary was invaluable; yet Garro Jones seemed intent on asking so many questions about them, especially in relation to costs and training. It was as if he had forgotten there was actually a war going on.

Wing Commander James asked a question in the House of Commons on 30 July 1941 of the Minister of Aircraft Production: how many pilots of the Air Transport Auxiliary service had been recruited in America at a rate of £1,937.17s 9d a year, free of United Kingdom income tax; what were the durations of their contracts; and upon whose direction and authority, and if with Treasury approval, such contracts were entered into?

The Minister of Aircraft Production, Lieutenant Colonel John Moore-Brabazon, in response said that the number of American pilots in the Air Transport Auxiliary was 162, and that their contracts were for a year, but there was provision for termination at any time on notice being given in writing. He also said that the contracts were entered into under the authority of the Ministry of Aircraft Production.

Wing Commander James further asked if his right honourable and gallant friend would take steps to have these extraordinary arrangements reviewed at an early date?

Lieutenant Colonel John Moore-Brabazon replied that no, he would not review the arrangements as they were at the time, because the position was quite clear. The American aviators were doing extremely valuable work, and that they were flying four-engined aircraft, two-engined aircraft, along with fast fighter aircraft and, although their wages might appear high to certain sections of the British public, the pay was in keeping with what they could expect to earn in America; and many of them wished to return there.

George Garro Jones joined in the debate by asking Moore-Brabazon whether the Americans were worth five times as much as British pilots who flew the same aircraft on active service. He further asked that the House at least be given an assurance that there would be no increase in the number of Americans employed on similar terms.

Moore-Brabazon replied that Mr Jones's first point had nothing to do with the question, and that the second point was that he, Moore-Brabazon, would have to move valuable aeroplanes about, and to do that he had to get the best aviators possible as he could not use personnel from the Royal Air Force.

Commander Oliver Locker-Lampson, Conservative Member for Birmingham Handsworth, enquired if the Americans were the best and worth the money that they were being paid.

Moore-Brabazon said that he was not suggesting nor did not pretend that the American aviators were necessarily better than British pilots.

In the House of Commons on 6 August 1941 Sir Archibald Knox asked the Minister of Aircraft Production what the annual cost of the Air Transport Auxiliary Force was and what duties it performed?

The Minister, Lieutenant Colonel John Moore-Brabazon, replied that it would not be in the public interest to disclose the annual cost of the Air Transport Auxiliary. The function of the Auxiliary is to ferry Royal Air Force and Royal Naval aircraft from the makers in the United Kingdom to storage and operational units.

Sir Archibald Knox, in response, asked whether it would be possible to get British pilots to carry out this work? He also enquired whether the organization came under the edicts and controls of military law, and could it not be a part of the Royal Air Force?

Moore Brabazon replied somewhat sharply that the same point had been discussed by means of question and answer as recently as the previous week. He confirmed that members of the service did come under military law and said that the Royal Air Force were far too busy to undertake such a role.

Mr George Garro Jones asked what the nature of the arrangement was by which the organization submitted its expenditure to the Air Ministry, by whom it was checked or audited, and upon what actual vote in the Air Ministry it appeared.

Moore-Brabazon replied that he required notice to answer all the points that Mr Jones had raised.

Mr Emanuel Shinwell, Labour MP for Seaham Harbour in County Durham, entered the debate by suggesting that the members of the House should be grateful to those 'American subjects' who were prepared to sacrifice themselves in the service of Great Britain.

Sir Archibald Knox continued the debate by asking the Minister of Aircraft Production what the weekly salary for Americans who were serving with the Air Transport Auxiliary, was; and how it compared with the salaries paid to British pilots of the same organization.

The minister referred his honourable and gallant friend to the reply given on 2 July to the honourable member for North Aberdeen, Mr Garro Jones, by his right honourable friend, the Secretary of State for Air.

Sir Archibald asked if it was fair that Americans who were serving with the Air Transport Auxiliary should be paid at a higher rate of pay than other Americans who risked their lives in the Eagle squadrons?

George Garro Jones asked the Minister of Aircraft Production, upon what conditions and financial terms were pilots of the Air Transport Auxiliary given advanced training at Royal Air Force flying schools?

The minister replied that the Air Transport Auxiliary had their own flying training school but, on a few occasions, Air Transport Auxiliary pilots had been given conversion courses on new types of aircraft at

Royal Air Force flying schools. He further explained that the cost of such courses came out of public funds and, in accordance with the wartime rules governing inter-departmental adjustments, no payment was made to the Air Ministry from the vote of his department.

In response Mr Jones further asked that, if facilities were available for the training of civil pilots, why did the Air Transport Auxiliary recruit a large number of pilots who received less than 50 hours' flying time prior to the closing down of the Civil Flying School?

Moore-Brabazon replied that that was where English pilots were acquired from, those who had completed less than fifty hours' flying time. He added that the reason why the Royal Air Force came into the question was that there were not too many of the new types of aircraft to be able to get British pilots accustomed to flying them, but that they would get used to them if they spent a short time training with the Royal Air Force.

Mr Jones responded by informing Moore-Brabazon that he did not quite get his point, and asked if he was aware that pilots who had amassed less than fifty flying hours had had no opportunity of completing their training to bring them within the recruiting regulations?

Lieutenant Colonel John Moore-Brabazon politely informed Mr Jones that those men would soon be wanted.

On 19 November 1941 a question was asked in the House of Commons by Mr Arthur Hugh Elsdale Molson, MP for High Peak in Derbyshire, and who at the same time was also a staff captain with 11th Anti-Aircraft Division who, during the Blitz, helped defend the West Midlands, including the raid on Coventry.

He asked the Minister of Aircraft Production in what cases the scale of pay for personnel of the Air Transport Auxiliary was higher than in the Royal Air Force; whether a special bonus was paid for landing aircraft on particular aerodromes in the south of England; and whether he would review those scales of pay and bonus so that they did not exceed the corresponding pay in the Royal Air Force.

Moore-Brabazon replied that, as regards the first and third parts of the question, it was not possible to provide a straightforward comparison between rates of pay of personnel in the Air Transport Auxiliary, a civilian organization, and the Royal Air Force, owing to differences in rank and conditions of service, involving such things as subsistence allowances, pensions and medical attention. The answer to the second part of the question was in the negative.

Mr Arthur Molson continued by asking his right honourable friend, the Minister of Aircraft Production, if he would give an undertaking that he would look into the matter with a view to seeing that civil pilots were not paid a higher rate compared with pilots in the Royal Air Force, whose skill was frequently higher and who were exposed to much greater danger.

The minister said that he would most definitely look into the question asked by Mr Molton, but could give him no guarantees on the matter.

A question was asked in the House of Commons on 4 February 1942 in relation to medical examinations for service pilots of the Air Transport Auxiliary.

Mr Gordon Hall-Caine, the conservative Member for Dorset Eastern, asked the Minister of Aircraft Production whether the Air Transport Auxiliary had the advantage at its various pools throughout the country of a fulltime medical officer; and whether he would arrange for medical officers to examine Air Transport Auxiliary service pilots each morning before they were allowed to transport aeroplanes, since this procedure would have the effect of diminishing accidents due to the human factor, and be a good investment for his Department in the saving of machines and man-hours, apart from the loss or injury to personnel.

In reply, the minister stated that medical examination was available at all of the Air Transport Auxiliary units, and that he had no reason to think that the present accident rate in the service had been adversely affected by any lack of these facilities. But that he was, however, having the matter re-examined in light of the honourable gentleman's suggestion.

Mr R. Morgan asked a question in the House of Commons on 9 December 1942 of the Minister of Aircraft Production. He wanted to know whether, having regard to the services rendered by the Air Transport Auxiliary Corps, consideration would be given in the future for the service to be known as the Royal Air Transport Auxiliary Corps, and that the pilots who served in it would use the royal crown over their wings, as was the case with pilots in the Royal Air Force.

Sir Stafford Cripps, the Minister of Aircraft Production, replied that he was fully aware of the excellent work that was carried out by the men and women of the Air Transport Auxiliary, and that he was already engaged in reviewing the status of the organization. He added that judging, however, by the customary standards which apply to such cases, he did not consider that he would be justified in adopting the course suggested by Mr R. Morgan, the Member for Stourbridge.

On 18 May 1943 Miss Irene Ward, the Conservative Member for Tynemouth, asked the Minister of Aircraft Production whether women pilots of the Air Transport Auxiliary received the same rates of pay as men.

Sir Stafford Cripps replied that it had been decided that. from the beginning of the following month, women pilots of the Air Transport Auxiliary who were engaged on full flying duties would receive the same rates of pay, rank for rank, as men who were similarly employed.

Miss Ward responded by asking Sir Stafford if he was aware how gratifying it was that the decision about female pay had been arrived at without any pressure from any of the female Members of Parliament.

Sir Stafford informed Miss Ward that he was grateful for her comments.

Mr Arthur Molson added to the debate by asking if it were correct that pilots who served in the Air Transport Auxiliary were paid higher wages than pilots who served in the Royal Air Force? Sir Stafford Cripps was somewhat muted in his response, saying only, 'That is another question.'

In relation to the increase in pay for female pilots serving with the Air Transport Auxiliary, Sir Francis Fremantle, the Conservative Member for St Albans in Hertfordshire, asked what date the increase in pay for female pilots would come into being, and would it be retrospective? Sir Stafford Cripps confirmed it would commence from June 1943 but would not be retrospective.

Just three months after this debate, Sir Francis died suddenly at his home, at Bedwell Park, near Hatfield in Hertfordshire. He was 71 years of age. During the First World War he had served in the Royal Army Medical Corps in Mesopotamia, reaching the rank of lieutenant colonel. He had also served as a medical officer in the British Army during the Second Boer War, between 1899 and 1902.

On 23 September 1943 a question was asked in the House of Commons in relation to whether men and women of the Air Transport Auxiliary would be entitled to war decorations and medals. Sir H. Williams asked the prime minister whether his attention had been drawn to the grievance on the part of those serving in the anti-aircraft units in the United Kingdom about not being considered by the Committee on the Grant of Honours, Decorations and Medals in time of war; and whether the matter was under consideration.

Mr Hewlett entered the debate by asking the prime minister whether he would consider extending the grant of the general 1939-1945 Medal to members of the Air Transport Auxiliary in view of the danger they ran from enemy air attacks whilst carrying out their duties, particularly at the time of the Battle of Britain.

In response, Mr Clement Attlee referred his right honourable friend to the reply the prime minister had given the previous day to questions on the same subject.

On 15 October 1945 the following, albeit brief, conversation took place in the House of Commons between Air Commodore Harvey and the prime minister, Clement Attlee.

Air Commodore Arthur Vere Harvey, Conservative Member for Macclesfield, asked the prime minister if he would state the number of decorations awarded to pilots who served with the Air Transport Auxiliary during the war; and whether he was satisfied that the outstanding services of many of these pilots, who had frequently delivered aircraft to battle areas, had been suitably recognised.

Mr Attlee replied that twenty-two honours and twelve King's Commendations for Brave Conduct, or for service in the air, had been awarded to aircrew of Air Transport Auxiliary during the war and that he did not believe that the scale of those awards had been inadequate.

Chapter Four

Female Pilots at Rest

One of the lovely moments about writing any book is when I discover something that I didn't know previously. This usually only comes into play when I am well into writing the book. But that's part of the joy of writing.

At an airfield at Hatfield in North London was an unusual pilots' restroom. The room itself was quite ordinary; it was sparsely furnished with just a couple of small tables and a few chairs, but this description is more about the individuals who occupied it rather than the room itself.

The pilots looked remarkably fresh-faced, as they prepared and looked forward to that day's workload, which they knew from previous days, weeks and months, was going to be a busy one. They are all sat around chatting amongst themselves quite calmly. A few were smoking cigarettes, not to hide any nerves that they might have had, but simply down to the addiction that goes hand-in-hand with smoking, I guess. A couple sat leisurely resting up against one of the tables whilst they awaited their allocations for the day.

They were all smartly turned out in their dark blue Air Transport Auxiliary uniforms, neatly pressed and not a hair or a piece of fluff in sight. A pair of tiny gold wings with a centrepiece that included the initials ATA was embroidered into the breasts of their jackets. The only thing that distinguished them from each other was that those with the rank of first officer had three gold bars on their shoulders and second officers had just two.

As the second hand slowly made its way around the dial of the clock on the wall, the time passed slower than the pilots possibly wanted it to, but they knew that any time soon they would be tying back their hair and changing skirts for trousers before donning their flying suits and parachutes. Although one of the four ferry pools of the Air Transport Auxiliary, those women all worked together; they were not split between the other ferry pools which were only made up of men.

Before long the waiting and anticipation were over, as Pauline Gowers strolled into the restroom, clipboard in hand, and handed out the delivery and receipt slips to her pilots. Her original group of just eight pilots, had risen to twenty-five as aircraft production had increased greatly, meaning that so also had the workload.

By October 1940, the work of the four transport ferry pools was fifteen times greater than it had been when the Air Transport Auxiliary began their operations.

Chapter Five

Air Transport Auxiliary Pilots Who Died During the Second World War

Below is a list of those men and women of the Air Transport Authority who were killed during the Second World War whilst carrying out their wartime duties, for which every one of them had volunteered.

The list of deaths is in date order.

Commander Douglas Stanley King: died 22 April 1940, whilst flying a Lockheed Electra aircraft when he crashed at Binn Uird, near Loch Lomond, en route from Perth to Heston.

First Officer John Taverner Wilson Clark: died 25 May 1940 whilst flying a Blackburn Botha Mk I aircraft when he lost height whilst avoiding houses and hit the ground at Horsforth, Yorkshire.

Third Officer Elsie Joy Davison: died 8 July 1940 flying a Miles Master Mk I aircraft when she crashed on the approach to RAF Upavon in Wiltshire whilst accompanied by Sergeant 745060 Edgar Francis John L'Estrange, an instructor serving with the Royal Air Force Volunteer Reserve, who also died in the crash.

Davison was the first female member of the Air Transport Authority to be killed during the course of the Second World War. She was 30 years of age, and at the time of her death is shown as living at 'Four Winds' Itchenor, near Chichester, having been attached to the British Overseas Airways Corporation which of course lives on to this day in the form of British Airways.

A few interesting facts about Elsie. She was born on 14 March 1910, at 221 London Road, York, Ontario, Canada, to Rupert Gustavus Muntz, a clerk, and Lucy Elsie Muntz, who had married in London in August 1906.

The 1911 census shows 1-year-old Elsie living in England without her parents and living with her grandmother, Minnie Isabelle Muntz, at Rotherley, Links Road, Winchester. In October 1933 she married William F. Davison in Chester, but they were already divorced by 1939. Despite this, Elsie kept his name rather than reverting to Muntz which she may have felt was too German sounding.

She qualified as a pilot at the London Aeroplane Club on 17 April 1930, flying a DH Moth 60 × 75hp Cirrus II, at which time she was living at 6 St George's Road, Golders Green, London. Her flying certificate number was 9053.

She was a very wealthy woman in her own right as her will shows that she left the sum of £12,747 13s. 9d. which, at the time of writing this book in 2019, was worth just over £700,000.

First Officer Herbert Roy Fields: died 4 August 1940 whilst flying a Miles Master I and having flown into a hill in heavy fog at Burnhead, Tweedsmuir, Peebles.

First Officer Sydney Edward Cummings: died on 29 August 1940 of injuries sustained whilst flying a Curtiss Mohawk on 26 August, when he was taking off from RAF Hawarden en route to Lossiemouth in Scotland. As he was taking off, the aircraft he was flying caught fire. He decided that his best option was to do a quick fly-round and land back at Hawarden but, as he attempted to land, he crashed and subsequently died of his injuries.

RAF Hawarden was only opened on 1 September 1939 and was used extensively during the Battle of Britain. It quickly gained itself a reputation as being one of the best training airfields in the country whilst also being classed as one of the most dangerous.

The airfield was also home to the RAF's No. 48 Maintenance Unit throughout the war and for many years after.

Captain Stephen Peter Reed: died 23 September 1940 whilst flying a Bristol Beaufort. He was coming in to land at RAF Dumfries, which was an

RAF Flying Training Command airfield during the war, when his aircraft was caught by a gust of wind causing one of the wings to hit the ground.

RAF Dumfries was certainly a hive of activity with 1,346 RAF personnel based there, including 445 WAAFs.

First Officer Luis Goncelvis Fontes: died on 12 October 1940, whilst flying a Vickers Wellington Mk IC. He was taking off from RAF Llandow in Glamorgan, Wales, when the aircraft stalled after one engine had cut out, causing him to hit a pole and crashed in nearby Llysworney village.

He was buried at Mapledurham Church, near Reading on Wednesday 16 October 1940. Prior to the war Mr Fontes had been a noted amateur racing driver who, in 1935, won the prestigious Jubilee International Trophy race at Brooklands racing course. He had also previously won the 24 Hours of le Mans race.

The newspaper articles which covered his death and funeral only stated that he died whilst flying on active service, but did not clarify with whom he was serving. There was no mention of the fact that he was a member of the Air Transport Auxiliary.

Mr Luis Fontes had an interesting life. Besides serving with the Air Transport Auxiliary and being a noted racing-car driver, he had also served a three-year prison sentence for manslaughter. On 6 October 1935, whilst in a drunken state and racing a car recklessly at high speed, some of which was on the wrong side of the road, in Coleshill, a market town in Warwickshire, he had a head-on crash with a motor-cyclist, Reginald Francis Mordike, failed to stop at the scene and, in so doing, showed not the slightest concern for his victim's wellbeing.

He appeared at Warwick Assizes on Friday 30 November 1935 in front of Mr Justice du Parc who, when sentencing Fontes, commented:

> It is by far the worst case I have ever tried. I don't know that I have heard a worst case. When I consider what you did on this day, it appears to me to be plain that this was not a question of whether you were likely to injure or kill anyone, but of how many you would kill or injure.

You behaved with a wicked recklessness for which there is only one excuse, namely that you were drunk. If I did not think you were drunk, I should say this was a case of manslaughter almost as black as murder.

Superintendent Horsman informed the Judge that Fontes' father had died when he was young and, on reaching his 21st birthday, Fontes inherited a considerable fortune. He had four previous convictions against him for careless driving, one for dangerous driving, and several for minor offences. For dangerous driving, he had been fined £5, to which Mr Justice Parq commented, 'Somebody thought that if a young man drives to the danger of the public and has plenty of money, it is a sufficient punishment to fine him £5.'

Fontes's defence barrister, Sir Henry Curtis Bennett, asked the Judge to remember the great mental anxiety that such a charge placed on a man, and suggested that one of the greatest punishments for a motorist in such circumstances, particularly for one who had done so much motoring, would be the suspension of his licence for life. Fontes had had too much to drink, and if some sensible person had stopped him from getting into his car a tragedy would never have occurred.

That was certainly an interesting defence by Sir Henry. Mr Mordike had been killed by Fontes's wanton recklessness in the act of driving his motor vehicle at high speed whilst he was drunk. His concern was that his client would, by having been charged with such an offence, be under 'great mental anxiety' and that if somebody else had stopped him from getting into his car there would have been no tragic event. It was interesting to note that at no time did Sir Henry say anything about his client having any regrets, feeling sorry, or that he should never have driven his car in the drunken state in which he was.

Mr Justice Du Parq sentenced Fontes to three years' penal servitude, banned him from driving for ten years, from the date of his release from prison, and ordered him to pay the costs of the prosecution at both the police court hearing and the Assizes.

I have not been able to establish exactly when Fontes was released from prison but, whenever it was, he never did serve his three-year sentence. Whilst incarcerated Fontes most definitely did not lose his thrill of speed. No longer having the ability to drive motor vehicles on his release, he turned to the thrill of speed-boat racing.

On Saturday 1 October 1938, at Newnham-on-Severn, in Gloucestershire, he took part in the final meeting of the season of the British Hydroplane Racing Club, winning two of the Races, both over the distance of 15 miles. The first victory was for the Springfield Trophy, which saw Fontes win with an average speed of 44.5 miles per hour. To put this into some kind of context, the second-placed competitor, Mr E. White, had his average speed recorded at only 21 miles per hour, under half the speed at which Fontes covered the distance. In a second race, an all-comers 15-mile event, Fontes won with an average speed of 45.5 miles per hour. Mr White once again finished in second place, with his average recorded at 22.5 miles per hour.

First Officer Leonard Satel: a Pole, he was killed on 28 October 1940 when the Bristol Blenheim Mk IV he was flying hit a balloon cable, which caused him to crash near Birmingham. He did not survive the crash.

First Officer Aaga Vademar Helstrup Laursen: a Canadian, he died on 4 November 1940, whilst flying an Airspeed Oxford Mk I when he flew into a hill in bad weather at Bynford near Holywell Flint, on a flight from Prestwick to Kidlington.

First Officer Amy Johnson: killed on 5 January 1941 whilst flying an Oxford to Kidlington from Prestwick when she was forced to bale out over the River Thames.

An article appeared about Amy in the Friday 7 February 1941 edition of the *International Women's News*.

> The world will remember Amy Johnson as a great airwoman, but those who knew her intimately will remember her as a fine woman. Her epic flight to Australia was the achievement of an inspired mind. Not to win personal fame did she set out on that long journey, but because the adventurous spirit

of her forefathers had stirred within her and here was an opportunity to help along a New Idea. She overcame physical frailty and much opposition, and with that thoroughness with which she did everything she planned her first long flight so that success should be no haphazard achievement, and failure nothing of which she would need to be ashamed.

The fillip which her flight gave to civil flying cannot be over-estimated. She certainly did her bit towards making the ordinary man and woman air minded in so much as she dispelled the fear of flight.

Amy won fame and suffered the inevitable price of fame. Indeed, she was an outstanding example of one who suffered from the wrong kind of publicity. Her private life became the happy hunting ground of anyone with a taste of exaggeration. But, as President of the Women's Engineering Society, she was happy in a world of women who could appreciate her for the quality of her mind and for the purpose behind her planning. Perhaps her real character is best summed up in the fact that, although she never quite abandoned the hope that the official mind would accept her as an air pilot and allow her to 'man' a fighting plane for the Royal Air Force, she yet accepted service under her friend Pauline Gower, Officer Commanding the Air Transport Auxiliary, whose tribute to Amy is that 'she was the finest pilot of us all'. One has to be big to serve willingly under another, when one is famous. Amy Johnson was big enough to do that.

Captain Herbert John Horsey: died of his injuries on 6 January 1941. Whilst flying a Mohawk on 2 January 1941 he hit cables and crashed two and a half miles north-west of the village of Wroughton in Wiltshire. He was a BOAC pilot attached to the Air Transport Auxiliary for the duration of the war.

Flight Lieutenant Dennis Brian Brooks: died 23 January 1940, whilst flying an Avro Anson when he had to make a forced landing at Southport due to a lack of fuel whilst en route from Carlisle to Hawarden. He died in the crash.

First Officer Ivan Christian Randrup: aged 26, and one of several Danish pilots who served with the Air Transport Auxiliary during the course of the war, died on 29 January 1941, the result of a self-inflicted gunshot wound.

Born in Whitley Bay, Northumberland, on 9 January 1915, he had acquired the love of flying before the outbreak of war as a member of the Kent Flying Club, where he qualified as a pilot on 21 June 1936. He went on to obtain his B licence in 1939 and, along with his cousin, Squadron Leader Michael Randrup, set up a small air charter company.

He is buried in Fettercairn Cemetery in Kincardineshire.

First Officer Francis Dean Carragher: aged 27, he died on 1 February 1941 whilst flying a Mohawk IV. He spun into the ground during an aerobatics display. Buried in Manchester Southern Cemetery, in Lancashire, his parents lived in St Joseph, Missouri, in the United States.

Flying Officer Leslie Arthur Phillips: aged 40, he died on 9 February 1941. Whilst flying Supermarine Spitfire IIA aircraft, P7960, he misjudged his landing, undershot the runway and crashed into a house in Meir, near Stoke on Trent in Staffordshire. He was buried in Southgate Cemetery, Middlesex.

Captain Percy Randall: died 17 March 1941 whilst flying a Hawker Hurricane from Henlow to Hullavington. He flew into high ground during inclement weather and is buried in All Saints' Cemetery, Maidenhead, Berkshire.

First Officer George Holcombe: an American, he died on 27 March 1941 whilst flying a Master I from Woodley in Berkshire to Prestwick, South Ayrshire, in Scotland. He flew into a hill in low cloud at Rottington Bes Head in Cumbria.

First Officer Robert Serge Loewenstein: a Belgian, he died on 29 March 1941, whilst flying a Blenheim from Speke, Liverpool, to Lyneham in Wiltshire. Both engines of his aircraft cut out a mile south-west of White Waltham in London. The airfield at White Waltham came in to being after the de Havilland family purchased a plot of land in

1928 and formed the de Havilland School of Flying, which opened for business in 1935. During the Second World War it was requisitioned by the Ministry of Defence in 1940 and became the headquarters of the Air Transport Auxiliary.

First Officer John Kenneth Bodinnar: died 3 April 1941, whilst flying a Hurricane from Langley airfield in Berkshire to the coastal town of Silloth in Cumbria. He was flying over Tarleton in Lancashire when he flew into the ground in bad visibility.

Langley was where some Hawker aircraft were produced after a new factory was built for Hawker Aircraft Limited on what had previously been farmland. Silloth airfield was opened in June 1939 and, at the outbreak of the Second World War, became an RAF Maintenance Command asset, housing 22 MU. In November 1939 it transferred to Coastal Command as No.1 Coastal Operational Training Unit and was used for the training of British and Allied pilots and air crews.

Captain Carill Stanley Napier: aged 34, he died on 29 April 1941, four months after having crashed on take off from RAF West Raynham in Norfolk, colliding with one of the station's hangars. Carill Napier was buried in St Michael's Churchyard at Halton, Buckinghamshire.

During the Second World War West Raynham was used by RAF Bomber Command. A total of eighty-six who took off from there never made it back home.

Irvin Trout Landis, Robert Eugene Fordyce, James Charles Torpey, Robert Alfred Lowell, Robert John Burden, James Seigel Wright, Kenneth Brown Collings, Robert Glen Smith, Ellis Gustav Friedrich, William Harold Nance and John Allison Woodall, were all pilots with the Air Transport Auxiliary on their way to Liverpool in England, having left Halifax, Nova Scotia, on 21 April 1941, onboard the SS *Nerissa,* which was making its fortieth wartime crossing of the North Atlantic. Also on board were 145 Canadian servicemen, a number of RAF personnel, Norwegian Army Air Service personnel, electricians, members of the press and a number of civilians. The *Nerissa* was built as a passenger liner and cargo steamer in March 1926 but, in 1939, was transformed into an auxiliary transport vessel with room for 250 passengers.

Nerissa was initially part of a convoy bound for the UK but left the convoy at St John's in Newfoundland on 23 April, before continuing on her own later that evening. On 30 April the *Nerissa* was sailing through an area of the Atlantic that was patrolled from the skies by a Lockheed Hudson aircraft of Coastal Command. The aircraft flew over *Nerissa* that evening, letting her know that the area was free from German submarines. Later that evening she was struck by a torpedo when she was about 100 miles off the north-west coast of Donegal, Ireland, by *U-552*. The survivors took to the lifeboats, which were in the process of being lowered into the water, when an explosion split the *Nerissa* in two, destroying the unlowered lifeboats in the process. The cause of the explosion was two more torpedoes that had been fired by *U-552* to ensure that the *Nerissa* sank. All those who were killed as a result of the attack have their names commemorated on the Ottawa Memorial. The British destroyer HMS *Veteran* picked up just eighty-four survivors.

First Officer William Noel Estes: an American, he was killed on 26 June 1941 whilst flying a Spitfire. Attempting to land his aircraft at Biggin Hill, he overshot the runway and crashed into a barrack block.

Second Officer Eric David Mills: aged 34 when he died on 28 June 1941, whilst flying a Magister. His aircraft was struck by another whilst taxiing on the runway at RAF White Waltham. He is buried in East Finchley Cemetery and St Marylebone Crematorium, in Middlesex.

Captain Harold Julius Hansen: died 24 July 1941 at The Radcliffe Hospital Oxford, having been involved in an accident at RAF Brize Norton two days earlier. He had been in an Anson that was struck by a Blenheim making an emergency landing.

His body was repatriated to Denmark. The Commonwealth War Graves Commission website shows his date of death as being 23 July 1941, and not 24 July as recorded on the RAF Lichfield website.

First Officer Francis Everett Bender: died 3 August 1941 whilst flying a Douglas A-20 Havoc. He was on his way to New Cumnock, Ayrshire, in Scotland, when he crashed into hills in bad visibility. He was buried in Monkton and Prestwick Cemetery, Ayrshire.

Captain Francis Delaforce Bradbrooke, Radio Officer George Albert Powell, Radio Officer Albert Alexander Oliver and Radio Officer Herbert David Rees were all killed on Sunday 10 August 1941 when the American Consolidated B-24 Liberator, AM261, they were in crashed into Mullach Buidhe near the head of Coire Lan and north of Goat Fell, on the Isle of Arran, having take off from Heathfield in Ayr.

Just four days later, Thursday 14 August 1941, and another tragedy befell the Island of Arran when another Consolidated Liberator, AM260, crashed when trying to take off from the wrong runway at Heathfield aerodrome, Ayr, before veering off the runway and crashing into a building.

Those killed included First Officer Walter Lee Trimble, First Officer Elbert Beard Anding, First Officer Philip Francis Lee (an American), First Officer Earl Wellington Watson and First Officer Martin Joseph Wetzel.

Second Officer Henry Edward Taylor: aged 37, died on 17 August 1941 of injuries whilst flying an Avro Commodore that had crash-landed at White Waltham on 10 August. He was buried in All Saints' Cemetery at Maidenhead, Berkshire.

Second Officer Jack Allan Marcus: an American aged 32, he died on 29 August 1941 when the Lysander III he was flying flew into a hill at Wigtown whilst en route from Lyneham to Prestwick in Scotland. He was a married man, whose wife, Katherine, lived in New Orleans, Louisana; he was buried in the Glebe Cemetery, Wigtown, Stranraer.

Second Officer Stephen William McFarland: a 24-year-old American, he died on 3 September 1941 whilst flying a Master II aircraft that crashed into the sea in bad visibility, two miles north of Drummore, Wigtown. His body was recovered and initially buried in the Glebe Cemetery, at Wigtown, but was later repatriated to America, where he was re-buried in Mound View Cemetery, Mount Vernon, Ohio.

First Officer Vincent George Govett: died 8 September 1941 whilst flying a Bristol Beaufighter IF that flew into high ground, three miles south-west of Capel Curig, Caernarvon. He was buried in Canford Cemetery, Bristol.

First Officer Richard William Purser: died 14 September 1941 when the aircraft he was flying, an Oxford II, en route from Ratcliffe to Burtonwood, crashed into the ground in bad visibility, four miles from Stafford.

First Officer Kenneth Meryl Seeds: an American, he died on 8 October 1941 whilst flying a Wellington from Hawarden to a maintenance unit at Aldergrove, when he flew into a mountain on the Isle of Man in poor visibility.

Second Officer Timothy J. Manley Corsellis: died 10 October 1941 whilst flying a Magister I. En route to Carlisle from Luton the aircraft stalled as he was landing at Annan.

First Officer Harry Wolf: died 28 October 1941 whilst flying a Beaufighter IIF en route to Atcham when the aircraft stalled, causing it to crash.

First Officer Isidro Juan Paredes: died 7 November 1941 whilst flying a Handley Page Hampden. He overshot the runway at Burtonwood and crashed. Originally he was buried in St Mary's Churchyard cemetery at Great Sankey but after the war his body was exhumed and repatriated to its final resting place in the Philippines.

Captain Walter Leslie Handley: aged 39, he died on 15 November 1941 whilst flying a Bell Airacobra I which stalled before diving into the ground near Fingland in Cumbria. He was buried in Yardley Cemetery, Birmingham.

First Officer John Graham Bergel: also died on 15 November 1941 but in a totally unrelated incident whilst flying a Blenheim IV that stalled and crashed at Oulton.

First Officer John Robert Baker: died 20 November 1941 whilst flying a Hawk Major which ran out of fuel and struck a hill near Priddy Wells, Somerset.

Captain Francis Joseph Bush and First Officer Elmer Edward Uhlich: both died on 23 November 1941 when their aircraft, a Liberator II, en route from Preston to Hawarden, crashed into the sea near Pidinny Hill, Stranraer, Wigtown Bay, after one of its engines caught fire.

Captain Bush was buried in All Saints' Cemetery, Maidenhead, Berkshire, whilst First Officer Uhlich was buried in the American Cemetery, Cambridge.

First Officer Ernest Edward Gasser: aged 31, he died on 7 December 1941, whilst flying a Hurricane that crashed into the ground at Button Oak near Bewdley, during a snowstorm. Although his parents and his wife all lived in the USA, he was buried in All Saints' Cemetery, Wribbenhall, Worcestershire.

Second Officer William Arundel Stewart: a New Zealander, he died on 9 December 1941, not because he crashed his aircraft, but because of appendicitis at Bursledon near Hamble. The following article about his death and funeral appeared in the *Hampshire Telegraph* on Friday 19 December 1941.

Air Pilot's Death

Mr William Arundel Stewart, of Dodwell Lane, Burlsedon, who died on December 9 following an operation, was buried on Saturday at the Bursledon Parish Churchyard. Mr Stewart, who was 26 years of age, was born in Matiere, Taumarunui, New Zealand, and had lived in England for about four years. He was a ferry pilot in the Air Transport Auxiliary and had just received his 'wings'. He leaves a widow and a baby daughter.

The funeral service was conducted by the Rector, Reverend C.H. Lewin, and the chief mourners were Mrs Stewart, Mr and Mrs F. Bevis, his father and mother-in-law, Mr Ben Bevis, brother-in-law, along with numerous other friends and family.

Among the beautiful flowers were wreaths from the commanding officer of the Air Transport Auxiliary, and Group Captain Barton.

Mrs Stewart wishes to thank all friends for their kind sympathy and floral tributes.

Second Officer Alfred Edward Green: a 25-year-old married man, he died 9 December 1941, whilst flying a Hurricane I. En route from the maintenance unit at Dumfries in Scotland to Cardiff, he flew into trees at Cockerham Road, Lancaster, in bad weather before crashing to the ground at Lunecliffe near Lancaster. He was buried in St James's Churchyard, Old Milverton, Warwickshire.

First Officer Joseph Stuart Wiley: an American, he died on 10 December 1941 whilst flying a Curtiss Kittyhawk I en route to Prestwick in Scotland from Speke in Liverpool. The aircraft never arrived and was presumed lost somewhere in the Irish sea. Neither the aircraft nor Joseph Wiley's body were ever discovered or recovered. With no known grave, he is commemorated on the Runneymede Memorial.

First Officer Thomas Williams Rogers: died 10 December 1941, whilst flying a Botha. He crashed on a flight from Sherburn to Hawarden, five miles north-east of Glossop in bad weather.

Second Officer Antoni Henrryck Gosiewski: a Pole, he died on 19 December 1941 after the Master III he was flying flew into a hill in bad visibility at Arrant Haw Fell, two miles north of Sebergh, Yorkshire, whilst on a journey from Reading to Lossiemouth via Shawbury. He was buried in All Saints' Cemetery, Maidenhead, Berkshire.

Second Officer David Aaron Marks, aged 32, an American, and First Officer Lee Leslie Garlow died on 26 December 1941. Whilst flying in a Hudson III they became disorientated in the fog and flew into the ground at Blacklaw Farm, Lowton, four miles north of Stewarton, Ayrshire. Marks was buried in the Jewish Cemetery, Willesden, whilst Garlow was buried in the American Cemetery, Cambridge.

Second Officer Richard Harry Winn: died 28 January 1942, whilst flying a Master I from Dumfries, Scotland, to Catterick, North Yorkshire. He flew into the ground in a forced landing at Baldoo Hill, Stainmore, Westmorland. He was buried in All Saints' Cemetery, Maidenhead, Berkshire.

Second Officer Percival John Collins: aged 29, died 29 January 1942 whilst flying a Hurricane I from Hanworth, Middlesex, to Dumfries, Scotland. He crashed in bad weather at Pen-y-Cae, Acrefair, near Wrexham. A married man, who lived with his wife, Janet Clark Collins, at Petts Wood, he was buried in Chislehurst Cemetery in Kent.

American First Officer Cletus Lloyd Park: aged 32, he died on 30 January 1942. Flying a Hawker Hind, he crashed at Eaglesham Moor, Renfrewshire. He was buried in Woodside Cemetery, Paisley, Renfrewshire, Scotland. Unlike many of his compatriots and fellow Air Transport Auxiliary pilots, his body was never subsequently moved to the American military Cemetery in Cambridge.

Captain John Lloyd Bebb: the 40-year-old American died on 30 January 1942. Flying a Mohawk, he crashed as he was attempting to make a forced landing at Pershore in Warwickshire after his engine had cut out. He was a married man whose wife, Laura Jane Bebb lived in Aberystwyth, Wales. John Bebb was buried in Capel Madog Methodist Chapel yard, at Cardiganshire.

First Officer Earl Lamar Renicker: a 35-year-old American, he died on 7 February 1942 flying a Hampden I. He crashed on the approach to Weston Parke en route from Preston to Thorney Island. His parents, Sherman and Delia Renicker, lived in Wichita, Kansas, but his body was buried and remains in Hale Cemetery, Cheshire.

First Officer William Johnston Elliott: the 24-year-old American died on 8 February 1942 whilst flying an Anson I. He crashed in bad weather at Buckles House, South Stainmore, Westmorland, near Kirby Stephen, in Cumbria. His parents, Gernard and Louise Elliott, lived in Chambersburg, Franklin County, Pennsylvania, but he was buried and remains in Hale Cemetery, Cheshire.

Second Officer John Alexander Nathan: aged 25, he died on 8 February 1942 whilst flying a Tiger Moth aircraft. He crashed into a Spitfire as both were attempting to land at RAF Ouston, en route from Witney in Oxfordshire to Prestwick, Scotland. He was buried in St Mary's Churchyard, Stratfield Mortimer, Berkshire.

Third Officer Bridget Grace M. Ledger Hill, 27-years-old, First Officer Graham Oliver Lever, also 27, and 24-year-old Cadet Betty Eileen Sayer died on 15 March 1942 when their Fairchild Argus stalled on the approach to White Waltham before crashing into a nearby house.

Bridget Hill was buried in St Peter Churchyard, Britford, Wiltshire. Her father was Major General Walter Pitts Hendry Hill CB CMG

DSO. Graham Lever was buried in St Mary's Churchyard, Broughton, Hampshire, and Betty Sayer was buried in All Saints' Cemetery, Maidenhead, Berkshire.

The Air Transport Auxiliary experienced three deaths on 15 March 1942, two of which involved Spitfires, but in separate incidents, after taking off from Carlisle. The third was Flying Officer Alexander Scott, who was 41 and flying a Spitfire V, when he flew into a hill by Breconside Farm just north-west of Thornhill, Dumfries, due to low cloud. He was a married man who lived with his wife, Lilian Scott, in Carlisle, and was buried in Dalston Road Cemetery, Carlisle, Cumberland.

First Officer Ronald Arthur Porter: 28 and flying a Spitfire Vb, he flew into high ground at High Lochenbreck, Dumfries. He was buried in Stanwix Cemetery, Carlisle, Cumberland.

The third Air transport Auxiliary pilot who died that day, was First Officer John Charles Fisher, who was flying an Oxford en route from Ratcliffe to Prestwick in Scotland, when he crashed into a hill near Wigtown. He was buried in Newcastle-under-Lyme Cemetery, Staffordshire.

Second Officer Nathaniel Addison Berry and Australian First Officer Thomas Charles Bray, who were flying in a Hampden, went missing between Kirkbride and Thorney Island. Nathaniel Berry's name is commemorated at the Golders Green crematorium, London; Thomas Bray is buried in All Saints' Cemetery, Maidenhead, Berkshire.

First Officer William Silver Edgar: the 35-year-old American died on 2 April 1942 whilst flying a Spitfire Vb. Flying at low level, he crashed twelve miles north-east of Dyce en route from Prestwick to Kinloss. He is buried in the American Cemetery, Cambridge.

American pilot Richard G. Miller and Canadian radio operator Nathan Frankelson, both died on 8 April 1942, when their Hudson IIIA, which they were flying across the Atlantic was lost and failed to arrive at their destination in the UK. Neither man has a known grave, but their names are commemorated on the Runnymede Memorial.

American John Burge Erickson: an American first officer, he died on 9 May 1942 when his Blenheim collided with another Blenheim just after take off from White Waltham. He is buried in All Saints' Cemetery, Maidenhead, Berkshire.

First Officer Alexander Ronald Leslie-Melville: died 2 June 1942 whilst flying a Hurricane IIB. He flew into a hill in bad visibility at Great Sled Dale, six miles west of Keld Richmond, Yorkshire. The aircraft was en route from Henlow to Silloth. He was buried in All Saints' Cemetery, Maidenhead, Berkshire.

Third Officer Joan Esther Marshall: aged 28, she died on 20 June 1942 when her Master I spun into the ground at Lyneham Road, Maidenhead. She was buried in All Saints' Cemetery, Maidenhead, Berkshire.

First Officer Stefan Czyzewski: married and 43 years of age, he died on 21 July 1942 whilst flying a Beaufighter. It flew into a hill and crashed at Glenyard Hill, Auchingilloch, Ayrshire. He was buried in Monkton and Prestwick Cemetery, Ayrshire.

Third Officer John Milne Greaves: aged 33, he died on 30 July 1942 when his Miles Master's engine cut out on take off at White Waltham, causing it to stall and overturn. He was married and lived with his wife, Mary, at New Moston, Manchester. His funeral took place at Chadderton Cemetery, in Oldham, Lancashire.

Second Officer John Richard Pruden: 33-years-old, he died on 12 August 1942 whilst flying a Spitfire V from Desford in Leicestershire to Prestwick in Scotland. The aircraft went missing en route, having last been seen at Girvan in Ayrshire.

A married man who lived with his wife, Eileen Pruden, in Redditch, Worcestershire, he has no known grave, but is commemorated on the Runnymede Memorial in Surrey.

First Officer Malcolm Goss Grant: aged 28, he died on 29 August 1942 whilst flying a Havoc that crashed at Abbott Piggott, near Bassingbourne whilst en route from Burtonwood at Warrington to Bradwell Bay in Essex. Malcom Grant was a married man who lived with his wife, Amy Grant, in Marylebone, London. His name is commemorated at Golders Green crematorium.

Second Officer His Royal Highness Suprabhat Chirasakti, adopted son of the late ex-King Prajahhipok of Siam: aged 25, he died on 12 September

1942 whilst flying a Sea Hurricane VC that flew into a hill in heavy fog at Eaves Hall Langholm, Scotland. His name is commemorated at the Golders Green Crematorium in London.

Third Officer and Flight Engineer Frederick Howard Moseley, 37 years of age, and Flight Captain Donald Ian Menzies Kennard, 52 years of age, died on 15 September 1942 whilst flying a Liberator II which swung on take off at Boscombe Down and collided with a hangar. It was on its way to the Air Transport Auxiliary's maintenance unit at Silloth in Cumbria.

Frederick Moseley was buried in St Mary's Churchyard, Farnham, Hampshire. He was a married man who lived with his wife, Lily Moseley, at Windsor. Donald Kennard, also a married man, is commemorated at Golders Green Crematorium.

First Officer Cyril Walter Morris: aged 30, he died flying a Spitfire V on 17 September 1942. En route from Hawarden in Flintshire, Wales, to Wroughton, Wiltshire, he spun into the ground at Saighton, Cheshire. He was buried in St Michael's Churchyard, Stoke, Warwickshire.

First Officer Edwin Allen Grundstrom: an American, he died on 7 October 1942. Accidentally fell down a flight of stairs and sustained fatal internal injuries. He was initially buried in the American Cemetery at Lisnabreeny, Belfast, but was subsequently re-interred at the American Military Cemetery, Cambridge.

Flight Captain Walter Mason: aged 50, he died on 21 November 1942 when the Hawker Typhoon IB he was flying, crashed into high ground in poor visibility, eleven miles south of Bunbury, at Brown Clee Hill, Burwarton in Shropshire. A married man who lived with his wife, Edith Mason, at Oxford, he was buried in St Bartholomew's Churchyard, Otford, Kent.

Second Officer Hubert James Dixon: aged 28, he died on 28 November 1942 whilst flying a Boulton Paul Defiant. Dixon was attempting a forced landing after his engine cut out and stalled, causing the aircraft to crash heavily into the ground at Timperley, Cheshire, whilst en route from Hullavington to Barrow-in-Furness. A married man, who lived in Gorton, Manchester, he was buried in Hale Cemetery, Cheshire.

Cadet Frederick George Bowles: aged 30, he died on 6 December 1942 whilst flying a Magister that crashed into the ground near Letchworth, Hertfordshire, some eleven miles south of Baldock. A married man who lived with his wife, Annie Bowles, in Newcastle-upon-Tyne, he was buried in St John's Westgate and Elswick Cemetery at Newcastle-upon-Tyne, Northumberland.

First Officer Norman Kenneth Rodway: aged 26, he died on 11 December 1942 whilst flying a Spitfire V that crashed into the ground on its approach at Newton Cottage, Farm Dyce. He was buried in Allerton Cemetery, Liverpool, his home town where he lived with his wife Kathleen.

Second Officer James Hector Stubbs: died 21 December 1943, whilst flying a Spitfire V at low level, resulting in it striking overhead wires, which caused it to crash three miles north of Chester at Mollington. He was buried in Allerton Cemetery, Liverpool.

Second Officer Irene Arckless: died 3 January 1943 flying an Oxford. Its engines cut out whilst taking off from Cambridge. She was buried in Stanwix Cemetery, Carlisle, Cumberland.

Patrick Morgan Trevor-Williams: 22-years-old, he died on 15 January 1943 whilst flying a Master III to Ternhill from Sherburn. The aircraft flew into the ground in bad weather at Bottom House, Ashbourne, Leek. Buried in Leek Cemetery, Staffordshire, he was the son of the Reverend Ernest Morgan and Clara Trevor-Williams, who lived in Puttenham, Surrey. His brother, Lieutenant Peter Trevor-Williams, also died during the war.

Flight Officer Alan Rees Colman: aged 42, he died on 17 January 1943 whilst flying a Hurricane IV which crash-landed, flipped over and landed upside down in the water, resulting in the drowning of Alan Colman. His name is commemorated at the Lawnswood Crematorium, Leeds, Yorkshire.

Ramchamdra Murlidhar Badhe: 38-years-old and from India, he died on 20 January 1943 flying a Hawker Henley that crashed in poor visibility at Methorpe, Westmorland, en route from Rearsby, Leicestershire, to RNAS Twatt, or HMS *Tern*, an airfield used primarily for training pilots on different types of aircraft. It was situated on Mainland, the largest of the Orkney Islands. He is commemorated on the Golders Green Crematorium.

First Officer William Byrd Lee Milton: aged 35, he died on 23 February 1943 flying a Beaufort from Edzell to 5 OTU Long Kesh in Northern Ireland. It crashed on top of Brownhart Law, Cottonshope Burn, a mile west of Makendon. William Milton was an American: initially his body was buried in Ware Episcopal Church in Gloucester before being repatriated to the USA.

First Officer Honor Isabel Pomeroy Salmon: aged 30, she died on 19 April 1943. Whilst flying an Oxford over Devizes, she crashed into high ground. She is buried in St Peter's Church, Dyrham, in Gloucestershire. Her husband, Major H.M. Pomeroy, lived in Westminster, London.

Flight Engineer Harold Frank Peter Waldron: 27-years-old, he died on 22 April 1943 flying a Catalina that crash-landed at Largs, Ayrshire. The aircraft sank before Waldron could get out. He is commemorated on the Runnymede Memorial, Surrey.

First Officer Donald Alexander Jameson: aged 33, he died on 24 April 1943 when his North American Mustang blew up and crashed a mile south of Bottisham in Cambridgeshire, having left No.12 Maintenance Unit at Kirkbride en route to Bottisham. He was buried in Christ Church Churchyard, Shamley Green, Surrey; his wife, Beatrice, lived at Reigate in Surrey.

Second Officer Mary Webb Nicholson: aged 37, she died on 22 May 1943. Her Miles Master lost its propeller and hit a house during a force-landing at Littleworth, near Worcester. She was buried in Greensboro New Garden Friends Cemetery, North Carolina, USA. It is unclear where she was initially buried in the UK before being repatriated.

First Officer Anthony Carpenter: died 21 June 1943 whilst flying a Wellington. Its engines cut out on take off from Hawarden, In Flintshire, Wales. He was buried in Newcastle-under-Lyme Cemetery, Staffordshire.

First Officer John Charles Shirley: aged 35, he died on 7 August 1943 flying a Grumman Wildcat IV that crashed at Pitbauchlie, Dunfermline, having taken off from Donibristle in Fife. He was buried in St Lawrence Churchyard, Meriden, Warwickshire.

Second Officer William Charles Lyndon Humphrey: aged 26, died on 20 August 1943 flying a Spitfire VIII that crashed whilst involved in a forced landing at Luckley Farm, Gloucestershire. He is buried in the Church of Ireland Churchyard, Whitechurch, Dublin.

Flight Sergeant J. Christopher Milliken: died 20 August 1943 flying a Fairey Barracuda that crashed close to Rufford bombing range near Mansfield, Nottingham, after the engine failed.

First Officer Stanley Eric Mitchell: 25-years-old, he died on 6 September 1943 after the Beaufighter he was flying stalled after take off and crashed at No. 19 Maintenance Unit at RAF St Athan. He is commemorated in the Pontypridd Crematorium, Glamorganshire, Wales.

Cadet Arnold Ernest Adams: aged 27, he died on 6 September 1943 flying a Hawker Hart that crashed on approach to RAF Thame at Haddenham in Buckinghamshire. He died from his injuries in hospital four days later and was buried in Oldbury Cemetery, Warley, Worcestershire.

Captain John Kilby Cummings: an American, he died on 7 September 1943 in a Consolidated C-87 Liberator when he crashed shortly after take off from Accra in Ghana at just after 1.00am. Nine other personnel died as a result of the crash, including eight members of the Royal Canadian Air Force and one from the RAF. All ten were buried in Chistiansborg War Cemetery, Ghana.

Royal Canadian Air Force

Pilot Officer J/27370 John Samuel Cram, 26, was the son of William and Maddie Cram of Morden, Manitoba.

Warrant Officer Class II R/110578 and Navigator Samuel Jacob Donen.

Pilot Officer J/26245 William Alexander Gardner, son of William and Lilie Gardner of Kelowna, British Columbia.

Pilot Officer J/29631 Ronald Cyrus Lounsbury, son of Cyrus and Kathleen Lounsbury of Windsor, Ontario.

Flying Officer J/10685 John Scott Maclean, 23-years-old and married. His parents, Aros and Winnifred Maclean, were from Toronto, Ontario.

Warrant Officer Class II John McCrae.

Flight Sergeant R/138274 Erle Donald Rennick was just 20 and his parents, Erle and Mary Rennick, lived in Vancouver, British Columbia.
Flying Officer J/26221 Eric Ogilvy Smith.

Royal Air Force Volunteer Reserve
Flight Sergeant 1028120 David Gale.
First Officer Deryck John Michael Martin: died 11 October 1943 flying a Hurricane I that had to undergo a forced landing, after its engine cut out and stalled, causing it to crash at Grange Farm Fife, five miles north of Cupar.
Flying Officer Maurice Gaston Emile Coutanceau: died 26 October 1943 flying a Hurricane that stalled and crashed ten miles east of Bees Head, while en route from No. 22 Maintenance Unit, Silloth, to No. 222 Maintenance Unit, High Ercall.
Second Officer John Shepherd: died 3 November 1943 flying a Beaufighter Mk X that crashed into the ground at the Worlds End, Llangollen, Wales, en route from Weston-super-Mare to Inverness, Scotland.
First Officer Laurent Frederick Ronald Brandt: died 23 November 1943 flying a Beaufighter that crashed into the ground at Cronton Mapley, in Lancaster, eight miles east of Liverpool. He is commemorated at the Golders Green Crematorium, Middlesex.
Flying Officer Alan Blair Dorrell: aged 33, he died on 1 December 1943 flying a Spitfire VIII that crashed in bad weather at Byron Hall Farm, Stag Lane, Lowton, near Warrington, en route from No. 6 Maintenance Unit, Brize Norton, to No. 18 Maintenance Unit, Dumfries in Scotland. He was buried in All Saints' Cemetery, Maidenhead, Berkshire, although the family was in Worcester.
First Officer John William Boilstone: aged 28, he died on 9 December 1943 when his Beaufort crashed at Kirkbride en route from Edzell to Melton Mowbray. The Commonwealth War Graves Commission website shows him as a Flight Sergeant Pilot with the Royal Air Force Volunteer Reserve and not the Air Transport Auxiliary. He was married and lived with his wife, Dorothy, at Blackheath, Staffordshire, but was buried in St Kenelm Churchyard, Romsley, Worcestershire.

First Officer John Dennis Hurley: aged 30, he died on 18 December 1943 in a Hampden I aircraft that crashed into a building as he approached the runway at Hawarden. He was buried in Mount Jerome Cemetery, County Dublin, Ireland.

Flight Engineer and Third Officer, Stanley Edwin Cooke and Stanley Richard Herringshaw both died on 23 January 1944, whilst flying in Beaufort from Fairoaks, Surrey, to Edzell. As the aircraft took off from Fairoaks, an engine caught fire, causing it to crash at Chobham, resulting in the deaths of both men. Herringshaw was buried in All Saints' Cemetery, Maidenhead, Berkshire, whilst Cooke's final resting place is in the New Cemetery, Willesden.

Flight Engineer Arthur Bird: aged 29, he was flying a Halifax II when he died on 24 January 1944. The aircraft struck high ground at Eel Craig near Bassenthwaite in bad weather and crashed to the ground whilst travelling from Kinloss to Kemble. He was buried in Edenbridge Cemetery, Kent, the town in which he lived with his wife, Vera Mable Bird.

Pilot Officer John Walter Hawkey: 23 and flying a Beaufighter aircraft, he died of his injuries at Cosford Hospital on 24 January 1944, the result of a collision with a Mustang on an unnamed airfield the previous day. The Commonwealth War Graves Commission website shows Hawkey as being from Ontario, Canada, and serving with the Royal Canadian Air Force. He was buried in Blacon Cemetery, Chester, Cheshire.

Flight Captain Bernard Short: died 24 January 1944 flying a Halifax II that struck high ground at Eel Crag near Bassenthwaite in bad weather while off course en route to Kemble from Kinloss. He was buried in St Mary's Churchyard, Ringway, Cheshire.

First Officer Geoffrey Maurice Firby: aged 34, he died on 5 February 1944 whilst flying an aircraft from Sherburn to Arbroath. He crashed near Winston in Darlington and was buried in Undercliffe Cemetery, Bradford, Yorkshire. He was married and lived with his wife, Doris Firby, in Horsforth.

Second Officer Jane Winstone: aged 31 and a native of New Zealand, she died on 5 February 1944 flying a Spitfire IX that crashed at Tong

Lake near Cosford, after the engine cut off on take off. She was buried in All Saints' Cemetery, Maidenhead, Berkshire.

Flight Engineer Janice Margaret Harrington: died 2 March 1944 flying a de Havilland Mosquito VI which crashed at Lasham. As Janice Harrington approached the runway, she came up short, quickly climbed to 150 metres before stalling, spinning off to the left and crashing into the ground. She was buried in All Saints' Cemetery, Maidenhead, Berkshire.

Flight Captain J. Herald Cordner: an American, he died of natural causes on 2 March 1944 at Prestwick in Scotland and was buried in the American Cemetery, Cambridge.

First Officer Dora Lang: died 2 March 1944 flying a Mosquito VI that crashed on the approach at Lasham, Hampshire, as it undershot the runway.

First Officer Charles Aiden Vernon Jeffreys: died 10 March 1944 in a Wellington II that lost height on take off and flew into the ground, just north of Aldergrove. He was en route to Shawbury, Shropshire.

Second Officer Kathleen Mary Kershaw and Captain Douglas Keith Fairweather died on 3 April 1944 whilst flying a Wellington that was lost somewhere over the Irish Sea during an urgent mission to collect a patient from Prestwick in Scotland. The following article appeared in *The Scotsman* on Tuesday 11 April 1944.

Air Transport Auxiliary Pilot Missing

Captain Douglas Keith Fairweather, of Air Transport Auxiliary, who is reported missing while piloting a plane, is the youngest son of the late Sir Wallace and Lady Fairweather, Faside, Newton Mearns. Captain Fairweather, who is a partner in the firm of Cruickshank & Fairweather, patent agents, St Vincent Street, Glasgow, was engaged in the last war as chief engineer on a minelayer. He became keenly interested in flying and on the outbreak of war, though over military age, he joined Air Transport Auxiliary. His wife gave birth to a daughter in London on April 7.

It is interesting to note that the article made absolutely no mention of Kathleen Mary Kershaw. However, the following appeared in the *Liverpool Echo* on Friday 14 April.

Flying Nurse Killed

Wellington came down in the Sea

One of Britain's flying nurses, Second Officer Kathleen Mary Kershaw, Air Transport Auxiliary, has been killed on air ambulance duty.

She was in a converted Wellington machine which came down in the North Sea this month while on its way to Scotland to pick up an RAF stretcher case.

Second Officer Kershaw was the wife of O.E.R. Kershaw, of Air Transport Auxiliary Headquarters. She had served as a nursing sister with the Royal Navy.

The pilot of the plane was Captain Douglas Fairweather, Air Transport Auxiliary, who has been reported missing.

His wife, the Hon. Mrs Douglas Fairweather, eldest daughter of Lord Runciman, gave birth to a daughter in London on Tuesday.

Kathleen Kershaw has no known grave, but is commemorated on the Runnymede Memorial, Surrey. The Commonwealth War Graves Commission website records that Captain Fairweather was buried in Dunure Cemetery, Ayrshire.

Second Officer Taniya Whittall: died 8 April 1944 as a passenger on a Lancaster I that had taken off from RAF Hemswell and crashed near Caistor in Lincolnshire. She was buried in St Margaret's Churchyard, West Hoathly, Sussex.

First Officer William Lionel Godwin: aged 30, he died on 30 April 1944 in a Mosquito that crashed just south of Lichfield in Staffordshire. He was buried in Weston-super-Mare Cemetery, Somerset, although his wife is shown as living at Markyate, Hertfordshire.

First Officer Francis Robert Marsh: aged 22, he died on 29 May 1944. Whilst flying a Beaufighter X from Sherburn to Lossiemouth, he crashed into the Firth of Forth. He has no known grave, but is commemorated on the Runnymede Memorial.

Senior Flight Engineer Royston Edwin Staniford and First Officer Claudius Echallier died on 8 June 1944, when they were flying in a Beaufighter X, which flew into high ground in poor visibility near the Mull of Galloway in Scotland. Staniford is commemorated at the Glasgow Crematorium and Echallier is buried in Brookwood Military Cemetery, Surrey.

First Officer Roy Leonard Egginton: died 9 June 1944 flying a Grumman Avenger II that went missing en route from Hawarden in Chester to Hawkinge in Folkestone, Kent.

First Officer Henry John Norman Rowe: aged 47, he died on 15 June 1944 whilst flying an Armstrong Whitworth Albemarle and is buried in Weston-Super-Mare Cemetery, Somerset.

Second Officer Thomas Maxwell Fisk: a 25-year-old Australian, he died on 25 June 1944 whilst flying a Mustang III that crashed into the ground near Petworth, Sussex. He is commemorated at the Golders Green Crematorium, Middlesex. His parents were Sir Ernest Thomas and Lady Fisk, who lived in Sydney, New South Wales, Australia.

Flying Officer Wilbur Washington Acton: a 28-year-old American, he died on 8 July 1944 whilst flying an Anson that collided with an Oxford and crashed five miles north of Hullavington at Robourne, Wiltshire. He is buried in All Saints' Churchyard, Maidenhead, Berkshire.

Flight Captain Eleanor Isabella Slade: aged 40, she died on 13 July 1944 whilst flying a Wellington that lost height and crashed after taking off from Little Rissington; it was on its way to a training unit. Eleanor was buried in St Peter and St Paul Church cemetery, Stokenchurch, Buckinghamshire.

Flight Captain the Honourable Margaret Fairweather: aged 40, she died on 4 August 1944 flying a Percival Proctor III. When the engine cut out suddenly, Margaret had to attempt a forced landing but crashed on landing at Shocklach, near Malpas in Cheshire. She was buried in St Peter and St Paul Church cemetery at Stokenchurch, Buckinghamshire.

Captain Frank Aston White: died 7 August 1944, aged 35. He was flying a Spitfire from Ratcliffe but stalled on take off, crashing into the ground nearby. He was buried in Newton Abbot Cemetery, Devon.

First Officer John Ludlow Glover: a 29-year-old Canadian, he died on 12 August 1944 flying a Barracuda. In the course of his journey between Kirkbride and Annan, the engine of his aircraft cut out, forcing him into a steep dive, from which he was unable to pull out. He was buried in Monkton and Prestwick Cemetery, Ayrshire. His parents, Frank and Violet Glover, lived in Vancouver, British Columbia.

Third Officer John Douglas Dale, aged 23, First Officer Thomas Frank Thompson and Third Officer Archibald Campbell Couser, who was 24, died on 17 August 1944, whilst flying in an Oxford aircraft. Due to engine failure, the three men had to endure a forced landing but, in the process, struck some electricity cables at Cranage near Holmes Chapel, causing the aircraft to crash. Dale was buried in Consett Blackhill and Blackhill Old Cemetery, Durham, Thompson in Streatham Park Cemetery, Surrey and Couser in Camelon Cemetery, Stirlingshire.

Second Officer David Martin Selby: aged 22, he died on 18 September 1944 whilst flying a Beaufighter VI; an engine caught fire before crashing into the sea two miles north of Lossiemouth. Selby, a married man from South London, was buried in Camberwell New Cemetery, London.

First Officer William Thompson and Dennis J. Richard Howell died on 6 October 1944 whilst flying an Avro Lancaster that was in collision with a Blenheim near Spitalgate, Lincolnshire. Thompson was buried in Hollywood Avenue Cemetery, Gosforth, Northumberland.

Third Officer Edward Easton Vergette: 23-years-old and married, he lived with his wife, Marion Vergette, at 'Clavis' Meols Drive, West Kirby, Cheshire. He died at Pear Tree Farm.

Third Officer James Milson: aged 31, he died on 15 November 1944 whilst flying a Seafire that crashed at Grange Hall Farm near the village of Carstairs in South Lancashire, en route from Kirkbride to Donibristle in Fife, Scotland, in a snowstorm. Milson's wife, Myrtle, lived at Mount

Dennis, Ontario, Canada, although he was buried in Tudhoe Cemetery, Spennymoor, Durham.

Third Officer John Platt Murphy: aged 33, he died on 15 November 1944 whilst flying a Barracuda from No. 15 Maintenance Unit, Wroughton, to Royal Naval Air Service Station, Dunino (HMS *Jackdaw II*), in Fife. He crashed in bad weather at Annesey North railway junction. He was buried in Cheadle and Gatley Cemetery, Cheshire, which is where he lived with his wife Alice Murphy.

Third Office Joseph Francis Wheelock: aged 31, he died on 27 November 1944. Flying a Mosquito he overshot the runway whilst trying to land at RAF Edzell, and crashed into the ground at Kirkbride Wigton. He was buried in Dalston Road Cemetery, Carlisle, Cumberland; his parents lived in Managua, Nicaragua.

First Officer Robert Graham Morris: died 3 January 1945. Flying a Taylorcraft Auster V, he crashed at Gatwick, and is buried in St Boniface Churchyard, Bonchurch, Isle of Wight.

Second Officer Thomas Blair Willans: a 41-year-old Argentinian, he died on 12 January 1945. While seated in a Wellington at RAF Dumfries, the aircraft was struck by an Anson that overshot the runway. Buried in Headington Cemetery, Oxford, he was married and, before the war, had lived with his wife, Daphne, at Carlos Pellegrini in Argentina.

First Officer Roderick Williams: aged 45, he died on 4 February 1945 flying a Barracuda in a totally avoidable accident. Williams was carrying out an unauthorised low circling manoeuvre in a residential area when he crashed into a house at Timperley in Cheshire. He was buried in Tomnahurich Cemetery, Inverness-shire. Inverness was his hometown, where he lived with his wife, Ann.

First Officer Gilbert Christopher Gould: aged 38, he died on 8 February 1945 flying an Argus I. En route from Waltham to Gatwick, he hit electricity pylons and crashed on houses at Headley near Leatherhead, Surrey. Gould is commemorated at Golders Green Crematorium. He had previously signed up for the Royal Air Force Volunteer Reserve.

First Officer Michael George St John Seelly: died 10 February 1945, aged 21. Flying a Miles Martinet I in bad weather, Seelly, crashed into a slag heap at Tankerton Colliery, Holytown, Lancashire. He was buried in Holmer Cemetery, Holmer and Shelwick, Hertfordshire.

The Commonwealth War Graves Commission website records for Seelly show him as being a Flying Officer (130960) with the Royal Air Force Volunteer Reserve. There is no mention whatsoever of him being a member of the Air Transport Auxiliary.

Third Officer Basil Frederick Wrightson: aged 23, he died on 13 February 1945. Flying a Spitfire IX over Opbrakel, Belgium, in bad weather, he lost control and crashed. He is buried in the Renaix Communal Cemetery, Ronse, in the Oost-Vlaanderen region of Belgium.

Third Officer Albert Edward Roy Fairman: died, aged 23, on 15 February 1945 flying a Mustang IV. He crashed at Wrightington, Lancashire, and was thrown out of the aircraft when it rolled over. Previously a Flying Officer with the Royal Air Force Volunteer Reserve, he lived with his wife at Clerkenwell, London. He was buried in Greenwich Cemetery.

Third Officer James Waldron Brown, who was 26, and First Officer Frank Hill, who was 32, died on 20 March 1945, whilst flying in an Anson I. Approaching RAF Aston Down, the No.55 Operational Training Unit, and also the Air Transport Auxiliary's No.2 Ferry Pool, the Anson was struck by a Typhoon, killing both Brown and Hill. Brown was buried in St Tudno Churchyard, Llandudno, Wales, and Hill in St Margaret's Churchyard, Hopton, Suffolk.

Third Officer Miss Leslie Cairns Murray, who was 28, and Leading Cadet Geoffrey Barnard Regan, who was still only 16, died on 20 April 1945 whilst flying a Hudson V that crashed into the ground at Popes Field near Taplow, Berkshire. Miss Murray was buried in Chislehurst Cemetery, Kent, and Regan, who was serving with the Air Training Corps, in London Road Cemetery, Staines, Middlesex.

First Officer David Russell Hayward: aged 24, he died on 21 April 1945 when he was flying an Argus I. The engine cut out soon after take off and the aircraft crashed near Lasham. A married man, Hayward was buried in All Saints' Cemetery, Maidenhead, Berkshire.

First Officer Reginald J. Richard Jackson: died 23 May 1945 flying a Hawker Tempest V that was reported missing after having left Aston

Down. It never arrived at its destination at Kirkbride and was believed to have gone down somewhere in the Solway Firth. With no known grave, Jackson is commemorated on the Runnymede Memorial, Surrey.

First Officer Ernest A. David Kempster, 44 years of age, a married man who lived with his wife, Hylda, at Leighton Buzzard and Second Officer Harold Race, 32 years of age, and also married and living with his wife, Dorothy, at St Anne's-on-Sea, Lancashire. At the time of their deaths on 22 June 1946, they were flying in an Anson I in Germany and crashed into the River Rhine whilst on a journey from le Bourget in France to Pilsen in Germany. Both men were buried in the Rheinberg War Cemetery in the Nordrhein region of Germany.

First Officer James Richard Burton: aged 30, he was flying a Blackburn Firebrand when he died on 30 August 1945. After climbing to 300 feet the engine cut out and the aircraft crashed to the ground and caught fire. Burton was a married man who lived his wife Phyllis in Selby, Yorkshire, and he was buried in Selby Cemetery.

First Officer Rosamund King Everard-Steenkamp: a South African aged 32 when she died on 19 March 1946, she was flying a Spitfire V that crashed at Pound Green, Upper Arley, in Worcestershire, due to engine failure, whilst en route from Hamble to RAF High Ercall in Shropshire, was home to No. 29 Maintenance Unit (it remained there until 1957). She was buried in All Saints' Cemetery, Maidenhead, Berkshire. Her parents lived in Moedig, Transvaal, South Africa.

The following article appeared in the Birmingham *Daily Gazette* on Friday 22 March 1946.

A Court of inquiry will investigate today a flying accident in which First Officer Rosamund Everard-Steenkamp, a wealthy South African serving with the Air Transport Auxiliary, was killed last Tuesday.

She was delivering a Spitfire from Hamble in Hampshire to an RAF maintenance unit in Shropshire. When near her destination, the machine crashed into some trees and she was killed instantly.

Mrs Everard-Steenkamp, the first woman to pilot a jet aircraft, was the widow of a South African Air Force officer, and daughter of a wealthy Eastern Transvaal farmer. She held the rank of Captain in the South African Women's Auxiliary Air Force.

A woman of many accomplishments, a farmer, an expert judge of cattle, a brilliant violinist, and a landscape painter, she was the first woman to receive a navigator's air licence in South Africa.

The slightly confusing part of this is that the Air Transport Auxiliary was disbanded in November 1945, so who Everard-Steenkamp was flying for at the time of her death is somewhat unclear.

Chapter Six

Those Who Served and Survived

In this brief chapter I have compiled a short list of names I have come across whilst researching this book of those who served with the Air Transport Auxiliary during the course of the Second World War. I do not suggest for one second that this is in any way a full and comprehensive list of those who served and survived the war, but simply a list of names I have so far come across.

H.C. Mason, Second Officer Air Transport Auxiliary Whitstable
Miss Pauline Gower, Officer Commanding
Mrs Gabrielle Patterson
Diana Barnato-Walker
Charles Bishop
Diana Faunthorpe
Alexander Agaronoff
Monique Agazarian
Patrick F. French
Kathleen Hirsch
David Hopkins
Percy Hudson
Henry Leach
Paul Longthorpe
Pamela Norman
Honor Salmon
Maureen Shiel
Martyn Steyor

Robert Tolworthy
Anne Walker
Peter Watkins
Arnold Watson
Alliston T.C. Hazledine
Robert Hugh Malcolm Sandeman
Ralph Canning (American)
A.H. Laureen (Canadian)
Ken Cleaver (American)
Earl Ortman (American)
Mr J.V. Wood
Mr Arthur J. Record
Mr Gerard d'Erlanger
Miss Roy Mary Sharpe
Captain P.C. Golding
Mr F.G. Gill
Mr C.S. Clarke
Mr W.F. Castle
Lieutenant James C. Quinlan
Miss Audrey Sale-Barker

Chapter Seven

Ferry Pilots' Notes

Every person who flew as an Air Transport Auxiliary pilot was provided with a blue A5-size notebook which provided them with important information concerning all the aircraft they could possibly be expected to fly.

The books were produced by the Chief Technical Officer of the Air Transport Auxiliary and were intended as an aide memoir for pilots, but only after they had familiarised themselves with the particular type of aircraft they were flying at any given time.

The 'flip-chart'-style notebook was issued 'on loan' to each of the Air Transport Auxiliary pilots, but only whilst they were authorised pilots working for the ATA. Each notebook was classified as an official document and was subject to the provisions and penalties of Section 1 of the Official Secrets Act, 1920, and of the Defence Regulations. Its transfer, irregular use, loss by neglect, disclosure of its contents to unauthorised persons or its retention or destruction after the termination of the pilot's contract with the Air Transport Auxiliary were offences under the Act. Any such breach of those regulations was an imprisonable offence, such was the importance of the notebooks being fully accounted for.

There were slightly different notes for each of the aircraft that were to be flown by the ATA pilots. For a Sabre-engined aircraft, here are some of the notes with which each of the pilots had to familiarise themselves.

Ensure that ground crews understand the special fire drill. There is a danger of sleeve valve seizure, therefore these precautions are essential. The engine should be run daily.

If it is known that the engine is not going to be run within 48 hours, it must be inhibited by the ground engineers.

Doping must be limited to 15 strokes, with a mixture of 70% petrol and 30% oil. If not then started, cylinder oil priming is essential whether or not a further attempt is made to start the engine. Engineers have instructions on how to carry out this operation.

For the Sabre engine there were four separate considerations just in relation to starting it. There was the 'Cold Start' system; the 'Engine fails to Start'; the 'Warm or Hot Start'; or the 'If Starter Bottle is Fitted'. For the 'Cold Start' procedure, there were eight stages to consider. If a pilot had to go through the 'Engine fails to Start' procedure, he or she had to check stages 4 and 5 of the 'Cold Start' procedure; repeat stages 7 and 8, and, if the engine still failed to start after three attempts, switch off, open the throttle, blow it out by turning the propeller, and then repeat stages 1 to 8 of the 'Cold Start'.

As if that wasn't enough to remember, there was then the 'Warming up the Engine' procedure, which was achieved in three phases.

(1) Allow engine to idle between 800 and 1,000 revs per minute, until oil pressure drops to below 100lb per square inch.
(2) Open up progressively, without exceeding 100lb per square inch on the oil pressure gauge, to 2,000 revs per minute.
(3) Maintain 2,000 revs per minute until oil temperature reaches 40 degrees C and a radiator temperature of 65 degrees C is exceeded.

When it came to stopping the engine it was a requirement that the engine should be idled for a few seconds only. Then the engine had to be opened up to about 2,000 revs per minute and cut off immediately by moving the starting lever to the cut-out position. Finally, the ignition and fuel had to be switched off after the engine came to rest.

Consideration and knowledge as to whether an engine contained a non-injector carburettor or an injector carburettor was also needed. Moving on to propellers, pilots needed to know the different types of variable-pitch propellers, of which there were four. Those were 'Counterweight, 2-pitch, or Constant-speed,' followed by 'Hydromatic Non-feathering, or feathering'; then there was the 'Rotol Hydraulic Non-feathering, or feathering' type; and lastly the 'Electric Non-feathering, or feathering'. To assist the pilots further there were detailed instructions on the procedures to be followed in relation to 'feathering' and 'unfeathering'.

Next in the notebook was the procedure that a pilot should follow in the event of an accident. It contained ten points:

(1) Note the time and position on map.
(2) Get responsible person to guard the aircraft and ask him to make list of eyewitnesses, while you ….
(3) Telephone the watch office at Service aerodrome or Air Transport Auxiliary Operations Room, whichever is nearer, and….
(4) State: Where you are and what passengers you have, damage and injuries caused
    Ask for: Your destination to be informed immediately, if you were signalled out, a guard for the aircraft, and a guard for the aircraft.
(5) Before finally leaving the scene of the occurrence, ensure that guns are unloaded before aircraft is otherwise touched.
(6) Endeavour to obtain written reports from at least two reliable eyewitnesses.
(7) Take possession of logbooks and loose equipment, if any.
(8) Collect more complete information on damage particulars for a sketch plan. Also note any damage to third party damage, and name and address of owner.
(9) Make sure the aircraft is left in competent hands and secured against damage from wind or rain.
(10) Report to duty pilot at Service aerodrome or Operations Officer Air Transport Auxiliary and carry out reporting and other responsibilities as set forth in full on reverse side of this card.

Note: If you have landed undamaged outside an aerodrome, you may not take off without the authority of your Commanding Officer or his designated deputy.

But that was not all: there were then several additional points for the pilot to consider:

(1) Report to the Station Duty Officer or Air Transport Auxiliary Operations Officer and give the following information.
   (a) Aircraft: Type, Mark, Number, Engine type and number. Check logbook to see if there is any secret equipment on board.
   (b) The unit owning the aircraft, if a ferried aircraft, the consignor and consignee, shown on the delivery chit.
   (c) Purpose of flight.
   (d) Full details of names, units and injuries to all personnel.
   (e) All possible information regarding extent of damage, and the causes of the accident or forced landing, including any relevant weather information.
(2) Ensure that a signal is sent reporting the accident to planned destination, ferry pool and, if a ferried aircraft, HQ 41 Group. Then telephone the pool.
(3) Hand over logbooks and loose equipment to a competent officer and obtain a signature on the delivery chit.
(4) Obtain a report, if relevant, from an officer representing the station commander on any defects of the aerodrome surface or airfield control and from an engineer officer, after examination of the aircraft, on any technical defect discovered. Tell him everything which will help his investigation. Make out a snag report if necessary and give him the top copy.
(5) In most accidents a sketch plan must be made showing such details as compass points, wind direction and velocity, runways and perimeter track, bad ground marked, and course followed by the aircraft in the air on the ground. If possible, have the plan endorsed by a witness.

(6) Do not leave the station until released by the station commander or his deputy.

(7) A written report on the occurrence must be made by your Commanding Officer and eyewitness reports, sketch plan, details of damage to property, detailed above, attached. If a written report has been made to a commanding officer other than your own, a copy of this must also be attached.

Each stage of the flight had its own checklist of vital actions to be carried out by the pilot. This included thirteen during take off, a further nine before landing and three after landing.

Air Transport Auxiliary pilots were provided with numerous different charts for different aspects of their journey. There were conversion charts for miles per hour into 'knots' and 'knots' into miles per hour. Fuel consumption for different lengths of flights, with remaining fuel levels if particular speeds were maintained. The same chart also allowed for extra fuel consumption as a result of flying into headwinds or crosswinds. There was a chart which contained the normal engine oil pressures for different aircraft, alongside an emergency minimum level, which meant a pilot only had five more minutes' safe flying time remaining.

There was a list of different aircraft flown by Air Transport Auxiliary pilots which included every conceivable piece of information needed to undertake and complete a safe flight.

The reason for including all the above information is to emphasise the extremely difficult job that these pilots had to contend with. For them it really wasn't just a case of arriving at a factory or maintenance facility, getting in an aircraft and then flying it to its required destination. There were procedures, check lists, *dos* and *don'ts*, things to do before the flight, during it, on landing and afterwards. All could be different depending on which aircraft was being flown, meaning that powers of observation and retention had to be 'spot on' at all times.

To emphasise their steadfast and continued commitment to the Allied war effort, here is a list of the different aircraft that pilots of the Air Transport Auxiliary flew during the course of the Second World War, many of which had improved variants, mainly because of differing or upgraded engines as the war progressed:

Albacore, Fairey (single engine; biplane torpedo-bomber)

Albemarle, Armstrong Whitworth (twin engines; bomber/transport/ glider tug)

Anson, Avro (twin engines; multi-role)

Argus, Fairchild (single engine; light transport/communications)

Auster, Taylorcraft (single engine; air observation post/communications)

Avenger, Grumman (single engine; torpedo-bomber. The heaviest single-engine aircraft of the war. Originally known as the Tarpon in British service.)

Barracuda, Fairey (single engine; torpedo-bomber)

Beaufighter, Bristol (twin engines; multi-role fighter/bomber)

Beaufort, Bristol (twin engines; torpedo-bomber)

Blenheim, Bristol (twin engines; bomber/nightfighter)

Boston, Douglas DB7 (twin-engine medium bomber/attack; see also Havoc)

Buckingham I, Bristol (twin engines; medium bomber/transport)

Buckmaster I, Bristol (twin engines; trainer)

Corsair, Chance Vought (single engine; naval fighter)

Dakota, Douglas C-47 (twin engines; transport)

Dauntless I, Douglas (single engine; dive-bomber)

Defiant, Boulton Paul (single engine; fighter/night fighter)

Dominie, de Havilland (twin engines; biplane crew trainer/communications)

Expeditor I, Beech (twin engines; light transport/communications)

Firebrand, Blackburn (single engine; naval strike fighter)

Firefly, Fairey (single engine; naval strike/fleet defence fighter)

Fortress II & III, Boeing (four engines; heavy bomber)

Fulmar, Fairey (single engine; naval fighter)

Gladiator, Gloster (single engine; biplane fighter/communications)

Halifax, Handley Page (four engines; heavy bomber)

Harvard, North American (single engine; trainer)

Havoc, Douglas DB7 (twin-engine medium bomber/attack; see also Boston)

Hellcat, Grumman (single engine; naval fighter)
Helldiver I, Curtiss (single engine; dive-bomber)
Hudson, Lockheed (twin engines; light bomber)
Hurricane, Hawker (single engine; fighter)
Lancaster, Avro (four-engines; heavy bomber)
Lancastrian, Avro (four engines; transport derivative of Lancaster)
Liberator, Consolidated (four engines; heavy bomber)
Lysander, Westland (single engine; army co-operation aircraft)
Magister I, Miles (single engine; basic trainer)
Martinet I, Miles (single engine; target tug)
Master, Miles (single engine; advanced trainer)
Messenger I, Miles (single engine; liaison aircraft)
Meteor III, Gloster (twin engines; jet fighter)
Mitchell, North American (twin engines; light bomber)
Mosquito, de Havilland (twin engines; multi-role aircraft)
Moths, de Havilland (single engine; trainers)
Mustang, North American (single engine; fighter)
Oxford, Airspeed (twin engines; crew trainer)
Proctor, Percival (single engine; radio trainer and communications aircraft)
Reliant I, Stinson (single engine; communications/trainer)
Sea Hurricane, Hawker (single engine; naval fighter),
Seafire, Supermarine (single engine; naval variant of the Spitfire)
Seamew I, Curtiss (single engine; reconnaissance/light bomber)
Sea Otter, Supermarine (single engine; amphibious observation/ communications biplane floatplane)
Skua, Blackburn (single engine; naval dive-bomber)
Skymaster I, Douglas (four engines; transport, designated C-54)
Spitfire, Supermarine (single engine; fighter)
Stirling, Short (four engines; heavy bomber/glider tug)
Swordfish, Fairey (single engine; biplane torpedo-bomber, spotter)
Tempest, Hawker (single engine; fighter)
Traveler I, Taylorcraft (single-engine light communications aircraft)
Typhoon I, Hawker (single engine; fighter-bomber)

Vengeance I, II, IV, Vultee (single engine; dive-bomber)

Ventura, Lockheed (twin engines; light bomber)

Walrus I, II, Supermarine (single engine; amphibian biplane observation/ air-sea-rescue aircraft)

Warwick, Vickers (twin engines; heavy bomber)

Welkin I, Westland (twin engines; high-altitude interceptor fighter)

Wellington, Vickers (twin engines; medium bomber)

Whitley IV, V, VII, Armstrong Whitworth (twin engines; medium bomber/ general reconnaissance)

Wildcat, Grumman (single engine; naval fighter)

York I, Avro (four engines; transport)

The above is the list of aircraft that Air Transport Auxiliary pilots had to fly at different times during the war. It is taken directly from the Air Transport Auxiliary *Ferry Pilots' Notes* and I daresay that they also flew a few others that were not mentioned.

Chapter Eight

James Allan Mollison

James Allan Mollison was born in Glasgow on 19 April 1905 and went on to become a pioneering Scottish aviator during the 1920s and 1930s, a time of rapid development in the world of aviation.

The Wright brothers, Orville and Wilbur, made history on 17 December 1903 when they made the first recorded aeroplane flight in an aircraft named the 'Flyer' which was piloted by Orville.

What first attracted Mollison to flying is unclear but, at just 18 years of age, he obtained a short service commission in the Royal Air Force, which made him the youngest commissioned officer in the entire service. After he completed his basic training he was sent out to Waziristan, which today is sandwiched between Afghanistan to the west and Pakistan to the east.

In 1925, at the ripe old age of 22, he was deemed to be sufficiently qualified pilot to become an instructor and moved to the Central Flying School, at Upavon aerodrome in Wiltshire, which was the main RAF institution for teaching pilots the required skills they needed to become military flying instructors. It had first opened for business on 12 May 1912, so by the time James Mollison arrived there it was already well established as a school of excellence.

Becoming an instructor at Upavon also gave him another first as, at 22, he became the youngest ever instructor in the RAF. He didn't maintain this role for long because, soon afterwards, he left Upavon to concentrate on civilian aviation. In 1928 he headed to Australia where he became an instructor in Adelaide with the South Australian Aero Club before going on to become a pilot with Eyre Peninsular Airways as well as Australian National Airways, where he met the equally famous aviator, Amy Johnson. So smitten was Mollison with her that he proposed marriage after having known her for just eight hours. She accepted the proposal and they married in July 1932.

As with most pilots of the day, flying was what drove nearly all aspects of their lives, and the opportunity of making a name for themselves was a big attraction because, if it didn't bring them fame and fortune, it certainly helped feed their egos by providing them with the opportunity of making them household names. One of the ways of doing this was by attempting to beat flying records. In this regard Mollison was no different: the buzz and thrill of flying were most definitely what inspired him and drove him on. During July and August 1931 he set the record for a flight between Australia and England when he completed the feat in a time of eight days and nineteen hours and, just seven months later, in March 1932, he followed that up by flying from England to South Africa in four days and seventeen hours.

As the 1930s continued so did Mollison and Johnson's attempts at breaking and making new records. Some they attempted together, whilst others were single attempts, including attempts to beat times that had already been set by each other. This placed quite a hefty strain on their relationship. In their marriage they were a couple, they were a partnership, but when it came to flying they were most definitely competitors. They divorced in 1938 after just six years of marriage. But, despite this, during the Second World War they both served in the Air Transport Auxiliary. As recorded elsewhere in this book, Johnson was killed on 5 January 1941 on an Air Transport Auxiliary flight from Prestwick to RAF Kidlington near Oxford after baling out of her aircraft which ran out of fuel and crashed into the River Thames at Herne Bay in Kent. But her death has always remained a mystery, mainly in part, because her body was never recovered. There were even rumours that her aircraft hadn't run out of fuel but been shot down in a case of friendly fire by the crew of an RAF aircraft after she failed to correctly identify herself. When Tom Mitchell, the man who claimed to have fired the fateful shots that brought her aircraft down, realised the following day what he had done, he was told by his senior officers never to tell anybody about what he had done. It was only in 1999, some fifty-eight years after those events, that Mitchell finally came clean about having shot down Amy Johnson's aircraft.

Mollison was involved in one of the Air Transport Auxiliary's more fortunate and unusual incidents when he flew as the co-pilot to his colleague Diana Barnato Walker. The Avro Anson twin-engine aircraft they were flying was attacked by a group of Luftwaffe fighter aircraft and, although struck many times by the German machine-gun fire, not only did it escape and reach its intended destination, but not one of the twelve passengers or crew onboard at the time was injured. They certainly rode their luck that day.

In June 1941 Mollison and a colleague from Air Transport Auxiliary flew the somewhat strangely shaped, twin-engine Burnelli UB-14 aircraft (also known as the Cunliffe-Owen Clipper, as it was built by that company in the UK) from England to Fort Lamy in Chad. The aircraft was for the exiled General Charles de Gaulle and was specifically fitted out for his personal use. It was a somewhat strange choice of aircraft to provide for such a high-ranking and well respected officer as de Gaulle. With only three of them ever having been made, there would not have been much scope when it came to the need for spare parts.

After the war Mollison was one of the Air Transport Auxiliary members who was appointed a Member of the Order of the British Empire. He also settled in London, purchased a public house and married for a second time, in 1949. At the relatively young age of 48, he lost his pilot's licence, when it was taken from him by the Civil Aviation Authority Medical Board due to his bouts of heavy drinking. Sadly, his second marriage, to Maria Clasina E. Kamphuis did not last, and he died on 30 October 1959 at the age of 54.

In Closing

There is not much more left for me to say that I haven't already said – an unusual ending to a book, I know, but there you have it.

The idea for the Air Transport Auxiliary was a stroke of genius. In a war that was always going to be a winner-takes-all affair, men were at a premium and to have a previously untapped source of manpower to use for such a purpose was a Godsend.

Early in the war, in the days and weeks between July and October 1940, the skies over London and the south of England played host to the Battle of Britain. During that period the Royal Air Force lost 1,173 of its aircraft and 510 pilots and gunners. This came just a matter of weeks after the evacuation of France, where once again pilots of the Royal Air Force had more than played their part in making sure that over 500,000 British and Allied troops escaped either being killed or captured on the beaches and harbours of Dunkirk, St Malo and St Nazaire during the months of May and June 1940.

During that period the need for British and Allied pilots was at its peak. If either the Battle of Britain or Dunkirk had turned out other than they did, that would have been the war in Europe lost and Britain perhaps invaded by the forces of Nazi Germany.

So, for every civilian pilot who flew with the Air Transport Service, one fewer front-line Royal Air Force pilot was needed to ferry much-needed military aircraft around the country.

To all the men and women who served with the Air Transport Auxiliary, during the Second World War, I salute and thank you for the service that you so willingly and bravely gave in our nation's hour of need.

Sources

www.peakdistrictaircrashes.co.uk
www.britishnewspaperarchive.co.uk
www.cwgc.org
www.raf-lichfield.co.uk
www.danishww2pilots.dk
www.airtransportaux.com
www.atamuseum.org
www.hansard.parliament.uk
www.wikipedia.org
www.ancestry.co.uk
www.aircrewremembered.com

Index